DUBLIN PORT DIARIES

Fighting Words is a creative writing organisation established by Roddy Doyle and Seán Love. First opened in Dublin in 2009, and now with locations across the island of Ireland, Fighting Words aims to help students of all ages to develop their writing skills and explore their love of writing. www.fightingwords.ie

'Port Diaries' and the series of workshops through which the stories of the members of the Dockworkers Preservation Society were gathered, is part of the Dublin Port Company's Port Perspectives Engagement Programme, which is intended to reconnect the story of Dublin Port to the story of the city, as part of the Port's ongoing development.

The Dublin Dock Workers Preservation Society is dedicated to preserving the industrial history of Dublin Docks. It was set up in early 2011 at the suggestion of the 'East Wall Buddha', Jimmy Carthy, (pictured above) to build on the work previously undertaken by Alan Martin and it has had some great successes. Jimmy passed away on the 28th February 2017 but we will continue with his inspiring words 'Keep going until the history is preserved'.

DUBLIN PORT DIARIES

Dockland Stories, Nicknames & Dictionary

A Fighting Words and Dublin Port Company Publication.

Dublin Port Diaries is published in October 2019.

© Individual authors 2019.

Design: Mary Plunkett
Cover Image: Aidan Hickey
Editor: Rachel Wernquest
Printed by Walsh Colour Print, Castleisland, Co. Kerry, Ireland

Fighting Words
Behan Square
Russell Street
Dublin 1
www.fightingwords.ie

Dublin Port Company
Port Centre
Alexandra Road
North Dock
Dublin 1
www.dublinport.ie

ISBN 978-0-9935827-6-9

DUBLIN PORT DIARIES

Dockland Stories, Nicknames & Dictionary

CONTENTS

Port Perspectives	9
Introduction	11
Contributors	12
Life on the Docks	13
First Days	24
An Average Day	36
Story Tellers	41
Dangers and Deaths	51
The Docks Over the Years	59
Fathers	69
Primary School Stories	78
Nicknames	83
Dockers' Dictionary	87
List of Stevedore Companies and Stevedores	91
Acknowledgements	92

PORT PERSPECTIVES

The Port Perspectives project was initiated as part of Dublin Port's Masterplan 2040. It aims to reconnect the Port with the City by celebrating their intertwined story.

A key part of Port Perspectives is a community engagement and education programme.

This has included collaborations between national cultural institutions and educational institutions on the one hand and city schools and community organisations on the other, curated by performance and visual artists exploring the theme of Port – River – City.

The results of these collaborations have been seen by many people, in exhibitions, theatre and music productions, workshops, talks, lectures, seminars and published material.

Fighting Words is the first Port Perspectives initiative to explore the theme of Port – River – City through the written word.

This Fighting Words publication brings together a range of stories, born in creative writing and drawing workshops organised in collaboration with the Dock Workers Preservation Society.

Lifelong dock workers of the Dock Workers Preservation Society generously shared their personal perspectives on work and life in Dublin Port and their stories inspired these new works.

Dublin Port is very grateful to all the participating storytellers, especially to the Fighting Words team of staff and volunteers. Thanks are due also to the National Print Museum for creating such a dedicated partnership and to Business to Arts for their role in helping to bring this latest Port Perspectives initiative to such a successful conclusion.

Eamonn O'Reilly
Chief Executive Officer, Dublin Port Company.

INTRODUCTION

The docks to me was an unknown landscape, a hidden world. Not having grown up in Dublin, it was a place where you went to board a ferry to England and beyond. Even today one may think of The 3Arena for concerts or of the many tech companies that have set up home there and the continual building and renewal works taking place around the area. But before that another world existed and I was keen to find out more.

'We've been telling stories all our lives. We didn't work, we just told stories.'

The above line is a quote taken from the first workshop held in Fighting Words back in June 2018. A group of retired dockers and their families came together, initially over a five week period, to work on their memoirs. Subsequent workshops took place in Ringsend and Irishtown Community Centre in November 2018. I was part of a team of volunteers who participated in these sessions. Each session looked at a different aspect of a docker's life. It was a way of providing a creative space, enabling the dockers to tell their stories and documenting their experiences of life on the docks, in order to preserve this unique and important chapter and have a record of a way of life that has changed completely.

Each evening we sat down for a couple of hours and worked together in small groups. We listened to these amazing words as they tumbled out. An anecdote started in one corner of the room would be picked up, added to, corrected or embellished and finished off in another part. Story after story poured out, in all shapes and forms, through conversations. A picture started to emerge, a language of new words became familiar. In one workshop led by Roddy Doyle, a Dockers' Dictionary was created. In another workshop we looked at the origins of the dockers' nicknames. The tools of the trade were brought in, the coal shovels and the hooks examined and handed around for us to get a sense of the sheer physical nature of the working environment and back-breaking work involved. Old photographs, paintings, poems and memorabilia were sifted through, and we also worked with an artist to create images and drawings associated with this work. What emerged was the trust and love shared between this group of extraordinary people, their sense of pride and sadness at the passing of this world: a tough world with few rights, many health issues, exploitation, harsh conditions but great comradery and a really strong sense of community.

In the following pages is laid down the results of those sessions. Like footprints in the snow, an image that stayed with me from a story told by one docker about the Russian ships coming in with cargos of timber with snow still frozen on the boards, and in the snow the imprint of bare feet of the women who had loaded the cargo back in Russia. As bad as things got, somebody else always had it worse. The footprints have long disappeared but the stories remain.

John Grogan
Fighting Words Volunteer

image
First boat to arrive after World War II

CONTRIBUTORS

Brenda, Declan Byrne, Margaret Cullen (Mairéad), Christopher Daly, Paddy Daly, The Sons and Daughter of Skipper Dunne, Richard 'Boxer' Elliot, Kay Foran, Mick Foran, John 'Hawkie' Hawkins, Jimmy McLoughlin, Willie Murphy, Paddy Nevins, Bernard 'Barney' O'Connor, Jimmy Purdy, Richard Saunders and John 'Miley' Walsh.

LIFE ON THE DOCKS

DUBLIN PORT DIARIES

This chapter illustrates the docker's daily work, the people that inhabited the docks, and some of the unique language of the dockers. Some of the following pieces were written, while most were told orally at Fighting Words Sessions.

A DAY'S WORK ON A TIMBER BOAT
by Richard 'Boxer' Elliot

When the crane lifted the hoist onto the wall, three men and a bogey[1] were there to take the hoist to the tier where there were two men to remove the timber from the bogey. So you can imagine the space they needed to hold the amount of timber from a Russian timber ship. For the consignment of a Russian ship you would need a couple of football fields – a long walk from ship to the tier. You had to make sure that you got a good bogey. You and your mates would walk a good few kilometres each day. If you had a bogey with a gammy wheel your heart would be broken. It's hard enough pushing over to the tier with the bogey full of timber without going over bad ground (bumps and dips). Hitting a bump would be like a ship hitting a wave; it would sway from side to side and your mates would have to steady the hoist to prevent it from falling. If your hoist fell you were in shit. First of all you wouldn't be able to take the rope off it because of the double turn on the rope. It would take ages pulling the timber through the strap and remaking it on the bogey. We had no forklifts then. Everything was manhandled.

The other two bogeys wouldn't swap for you, so the hoist would hang on the wall until you put it on your bogey. Now here is what made everything very hard for you. The time elapsed gave the men in the hatch the time to put more timber into the hoist. That would slow you down and they could work at their ease, and all the pressure was on you not the other two bogeys, just yours. That is why everything had to be right.

[1] *Four-wheeled trolley*

image opposite

Dockers discharging poles for the E.S.B. (Electricity Supply Board)

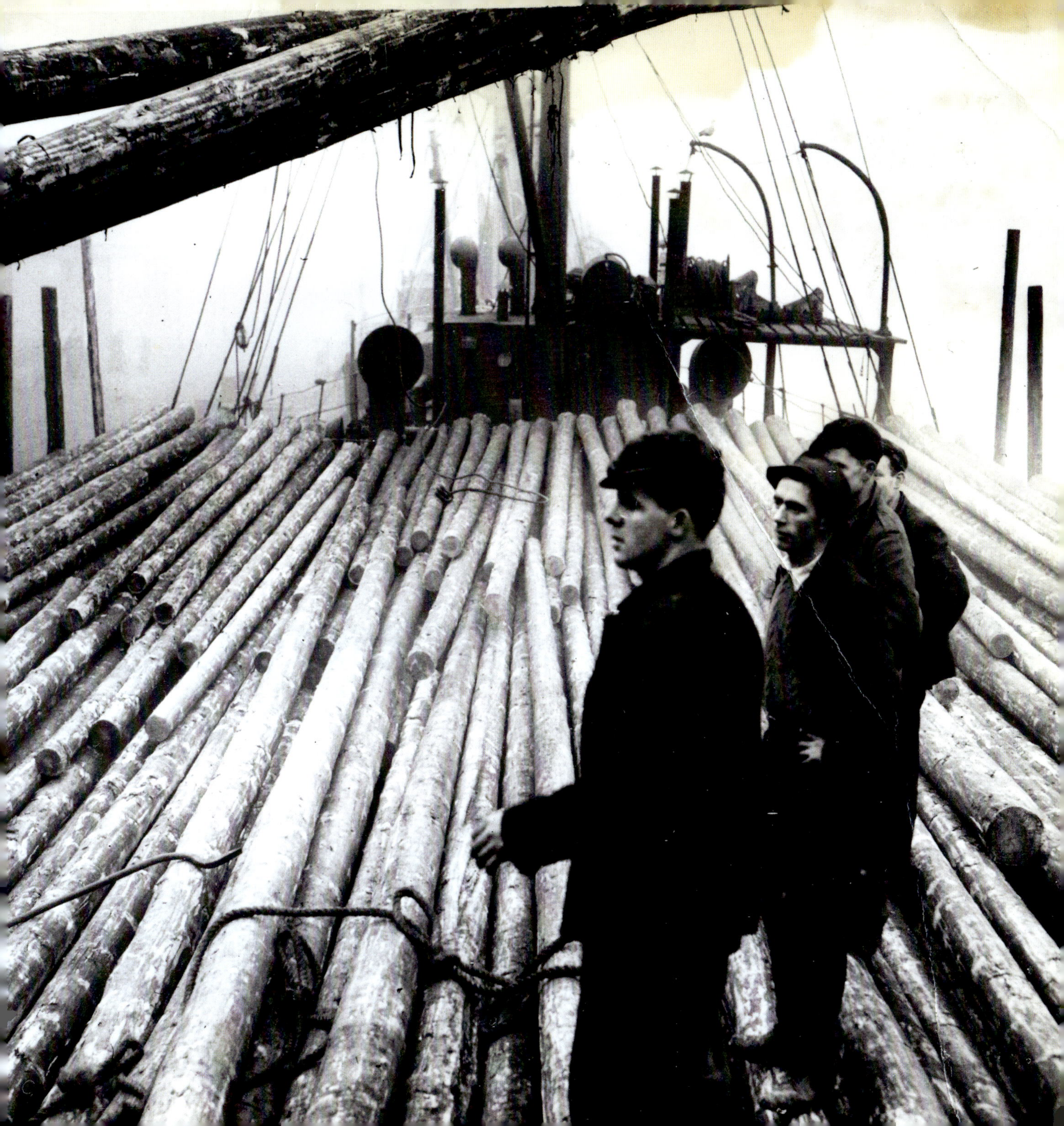

WHAT WAS A SINGER-OUT?
by Paddy Daly

The singer-out was a docker that stood on the deck of the ship giving instructions/directions to the craneman, by voice, or regulation hand signals. Regulation hand signals are pretty much internationally recognised and can, and have been used to transcend/overcome a language problem. The craneman, as part of his training, would be familiar with these signals. Singing out is a metaphor, or dock parlance for shouting out orders, warnings, instructions, or signalling to the craneman, or to the men in the hold of the ship.

These were men that worked for many, many years on the docks. Now at an advanced age, and beyond hard manual labour, singing out was an opportunity to extend their working life on the docks. Because of their many years' service and experience, these older men were ideal for this very important, accident prevention job. For example: Because of their knowledge of slinging cargo correctly over the years, should they observe a sling or hoist that they believed was unsafe, they would refuse to have the crane lift above men's heads. A sharp exchange of expletives might follow, but to these old warriors, this was water off a duck.

There were others with disabilities of one kind or another (some industry related) that could do nothing else but sing out. I remember one man, an amputee (only one leg) he was a regular singer-out. In the main it would be old dockers that were past heavy manual labour.

Each company would have its own regular singer-outs. Sometimes through nepotism, but mostly it would be men that had worked for the company for many years. The quid-pro-quo in all of this for the company/foreman was you had a company man or relative in a key position. Very useful with regard to feedback. Keeping you aware or informed of any on the job malpractice happening in your absence.

The singer-out, whilst being an integral part of the gang, was paid less than the rest of the men. The singer-out was paid a flat day's pay, which could be significantly less than the rest. He did not get paid for tonnage output, waiting time, dunnage hours, ships hours, shifting cargo, nor other bonuses paid to the gang. This, on the face of it, might seem unfair, but in reality, it was this and the fact that you could not leave your work (spell off). This made the singer-out job unattractive to the younger men, and ensured that the old men and disabled would have a job. It was so important that the singer-out gets it right. He is, after all, the eyes and ears of the craneman.

FROM THE SESSIONS

'Ah there was some good stevedores[2]. They'd eventually call you. They were fair in that sense. If you let something fall or done damage they may leave you a week idle just to chastise you. And stevedores kept to themselves. Oh, stevedores had their special place in the snugs in the pubs. They didn't mix with dockers. Because it would be bloody hard if they went out and drank with dockers … they'd have this fella and that fella asking for a job. People would even go to their wives to get their husband to give their sons a job and all. There was plenty of poverty at that time and you couldn't very well blame them. Their doors would be nearly tore down, men looking for jobs. Men currying favour with them, they'd leave a "hanger" at the public house for the stevedores. A hanger was a baby Power's Whiskey and there was a little corkscrew on the top of it and they used to hang it at a counter for the stevedores. But a stevedore might get on to him and kick him.'

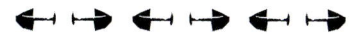

'Northside stevedores always gave northside men the first preference for jobs. And the Ringsend men then, naturally, give their men the jobs. Human nature and politics. And there'd be jealousy. Now Ringsend, they were a little village. Very clannish. They were always suspicious of strangers. And if a girl married a fella from the city you wouldn't get a house in Ringsend! She'd have to get out. It was a tradition. And there was certain docker gangs fighting one another, like Ringsend and the northside crowd, or parish-minded people. Like it could be three or four brothers from each side, a family. You know, that sort of thing. And if anyone interfered, some other fella would take him on! Now rows in them days, there was no knives or bottles. I remember some trouble with bats, but it was a fair fight. But then they'd have a pint together.'

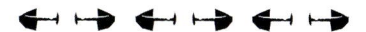

'Dockers, they worked and drank. They were paid every job, every day. They'd enjoy

[2] *Men in charge of assigning jobs to dockers*

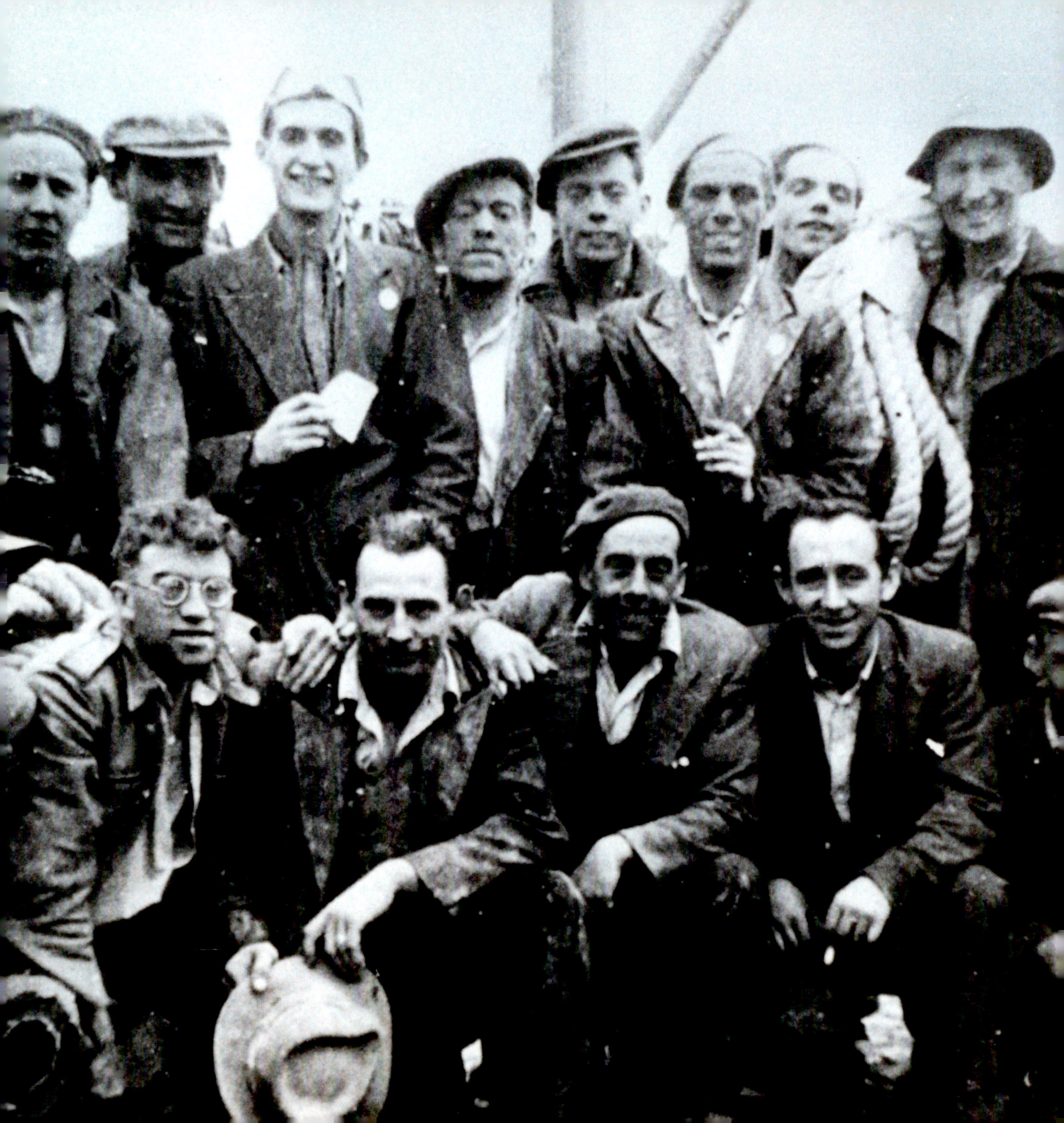

LIFE ON THE DOCKS

themselves that one night. Oh Christ, dockers only lived for the one day. They were millionaires when they were working, that night. But they may be paupers for the rest of the week. Now tradesmen had their own corner in the pub and the dockers would be on the other side. Oh, they'd talk to one another, but they'd never have a drink. Tradesmen had their place in the pub, same as stevedores. They didn't drink with dockers. Dockers had a very bad name, some of them. Terrible rough characters. It was probably that. Ah, but dockers was some of the finest men in the world.'

⇐ ⇒ ⇐ ⇒ ⇐ ⇒

'Now I was single at the time and maybe got fifteen shillings a day. That would be alright if you were getting it every night, but you might only get it two, three days of the week. Your drink could be put on credit – put it on the "tick" or the "slate". They were very honest and the first job they got, they paid. And if a docker died and the family wasn't insured, the publican would bury you. Great sense of community. He'd say, "go up and get the undertaker – I'll pay for it." And you'd pay him maybe a pound a week after that. And they'd carry him, the coffin, on their shoulders three times around the chapel and stop in front of his house for a couple of minutes.'

⇐ ⇒ ⇐ ⇒ ⇐ ⇒

'After the war, in 1946, there was 2,000 dockers here in the Dublin port. Then the buttons[3] came out, the union thing. There was 650 button men and he [the stevedore] had to employ them first. The others were in the union but they was "casuals" – hadn't got the button. The first 650 buttons were given [based] on their years of service on the docks. From that onwards you had to be a son. When a man died, he gave it to him [his son]. It was left with the mother to choose the son. Me own son went down there and didn't get a button because there was no buttons available. That was the poorest form of seniority in the world.'

3
Buttons signified priority; button men were picked before men without buttons

image opposite
The famous Carrick 'House Gang'

'And there were some prostitutes on the docks. Most of them were country girls, and a couple of Dublin girls as well. They used to pick up the sailor and go off drinking and then go aboard the ship with him. Now we had two – I always used to call them "two ladies" – they were unfortunates, and they used to have a stand at the back of the Gas Company. There was a long, dark walk and a wall there. These two ladies were well known and pretty good looking too, although they were around forty or forty-five years old. And anybody who felt like going down there they just paid a shilling, that's all they charged. They earned their living for years at one shilling.'

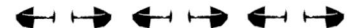

⇐ ⇒ ⇐ ⇒ ⇐ ⇒

'Stevedores had great power, terrific power. A hundred, two hundred men might turn up for a read. And for maybe sixty-three jobs. He'd get on the bridge of the ship and we stood on the wall. The family of the stevedore would be the first called – nepotism from the very word go. Now after that, he'd call whoever he liked. Or the best workers. They all had favourites. They knew all the names. Stevedores would call you from their mind. No lists. And stevedores were very strong, very independent in their ways. Physically and mentally very strong. And they walked very tall in their attitude. They always looked different from the ordinary dockers in the way they dressed. They'd wear beautiful suits and ties, and a big gold watch and chain, a soft hat and a trilby. They were done up to the nines! But he'd call whoever he liked and bribing went on. If a stevedore came to a pub, they used to do it in an undercover way. They'd leave a small whiskey for him, or a "ball of malt" they used to call it in them days. Well, that was for us to get a job! Stevedores would take that.'

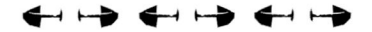

⇐ ⇒ ⇐ ⇒ ⇐ ⇒

'At reads, men had it in their minds that there was something at home wanting on that table and if they didn't get a job that just put them down in the depths. It's true, you could see the tears in their eyes. And they'd run from one read to another cause there'd be reads for other ships. Like some of them we'd call "cross-country runners" cause they would run that fast to get to another read. As soon as one read was over, you could see them run. They were gone. And there were some men that had an old bike and they'd jump on that and had an advantage. Many a time my name didn't get called at reads. I felt down in the dumps, really down in the dumps. You never got a smooth run on the docks. It was a way of life.'

'Dockers were big drinkers. The work was so hard that drink, it was a beverage to build up the sweat you were losing during the day. Plain porter, that was the docker's drink. The plain pint. It was 8p. I seen men drinking, honestly, fifteen to twenty pints in the one day in maybe two sessions. And I'm telling you, they wouldn't be drunk! They'd know what they'd be talking about and be singing old songs. Now whiskey was always 3p dearer. In them days whiskey was a gentleman's drink. Or a tradesman. And you'd never see a tradesman drinking with a docker. We were always looked down on by tradesmen as the poor relations. . . always downgraded.'

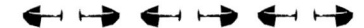

'Now, when Guinness's discharged their barrels after being emptied in, say, London or Manchester, Liverpool – they'd bring them back and load up empties there at City Quay. Big casks and small casks. Now the "hoggers" – hoggers was men looking for free drink – they'd shake the barrels. They were knockabouts. And dockers often done it. Yeah, a docker often went and had a sip. "Fond to drink it out of an old boot," we'd say. They'd shake the barrel and hear it and say, "we have one!" So they'd put it up on top of another barrel and tip the porter into the rim of the barrel and then they'd go down and suck it up. Now they always had the red raddle that goes around the rim of the barrel. Well, this red raddle used to go into the porter and when they'd finished up their mouths would be red, like if they were painted. And you'd say, "there's a hogger," cause the red raddle would be on his lips.'

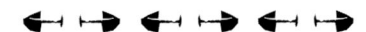

'I enjoyed working the bag boats – say, cocoa beans. And the smaller bags of sugar, the eight-stone and ten-stone bags. But I worked 24 stone bags of sugar. Me and my mate would lift them into a rope. And it was always a pleasure to work in your skin working timber. Because the job was so clean. Nothing to get on you, no dust or anything. And back then the two-masted schooners, they'd be bringing in the red bricks from Chester River in England. We used to take them by hand and pitch them out of the boat. Two bricks at a time. I'd be in the hole and I'd pitch two bricks at a time and you'd catch them and throw them up to the next man on his platform. We were experts at throwing them and catching. And the bricks never separated going up. I done that with bricks and slates as well.'

'Dockers was always proud and independent. I worked nearly fifty years in it. I wouldn't have any other way of life. I was always happy at it and I reared a good family. I got layoffs, but I was always handy and could mend a pair of boots or paint a ceiling. I've no regrets to tell you the truth. I was happy as Larry because it was like a beehive down there, and you'd listen to them all night telling yarns in the pubs. But I retired in 1979 and I don't believe I was twice down there since. It's sad. . . very sad.'

AN ODE TO BAG HOOKS

Bag hooks were hooks with multiple prongs that were specifically designed to pick up and move bags without tearing them.

'You wouldn't use [a different type of hook] for bags, or they'd rip.'

'There was an abundance of hooks. There were enough people wanting to get away from that class of work. And as you became established, you could nearly pick them. I had three uncles and they supplied me with all the hooks I needed. There was no such thing as having a locker room where you could keep those things. So if you had a friend with a car, everyone went to the one car and got their hooks out of it. There were very few with cars in the sixties. I had a little bike. I got the box on the back of it. And I had several of them in that. Even I got established with power. Then I became the person loaning the hooks. It was just a progression I suppose. Some of the guys could go home and collect the hooks.'

'The American trade unions, the Australian trade unions, the European trade unions – all used the hook as a symbol of solidarity.'

'I love the symbolism. The hooks and the work were hard (and that's why I avoided it.) All this work was done, and there was injuries.'

'It was a symbol. It was much more than a tool.'

image opposite
Linocuts cut and printed at the National Print Museum

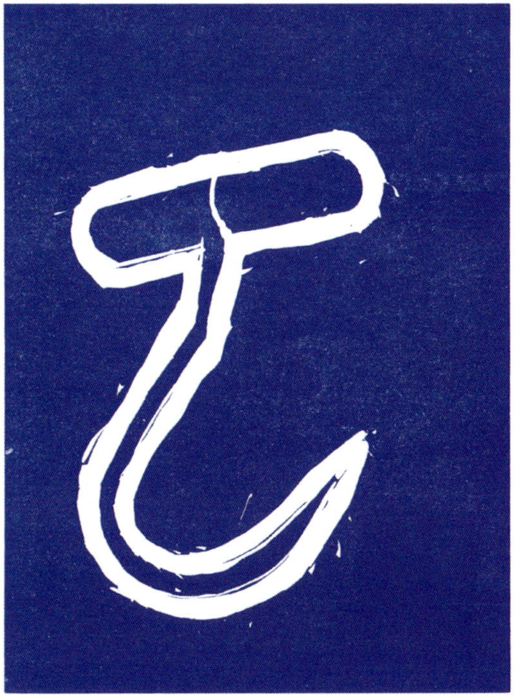
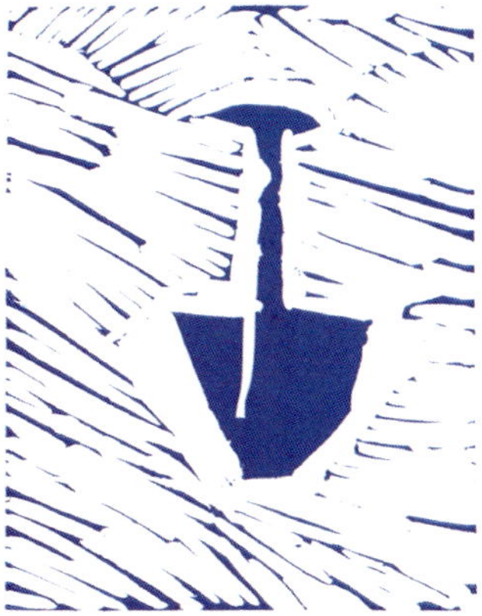
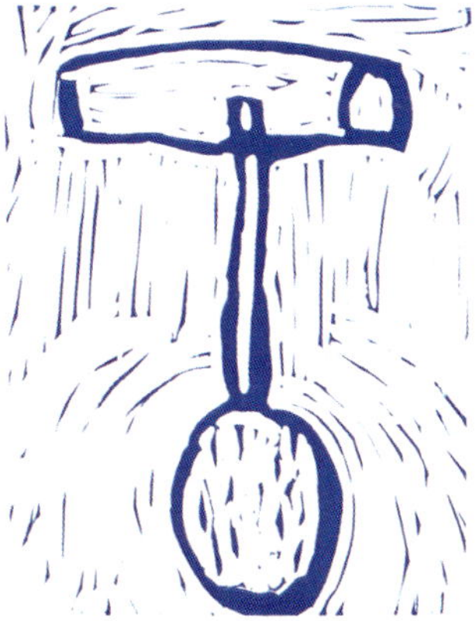
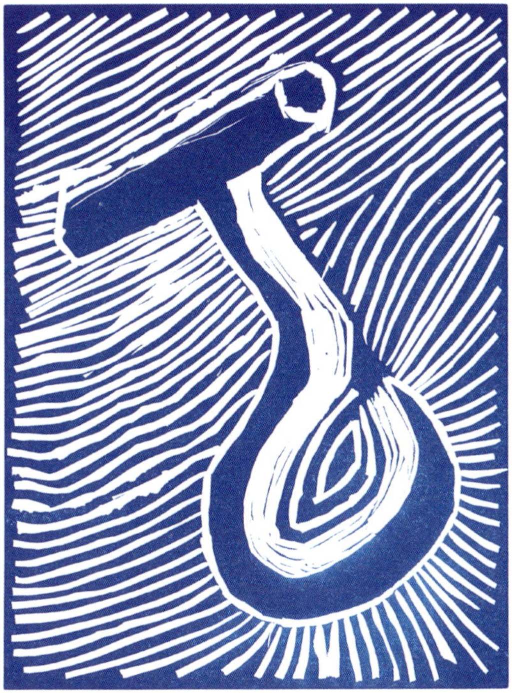
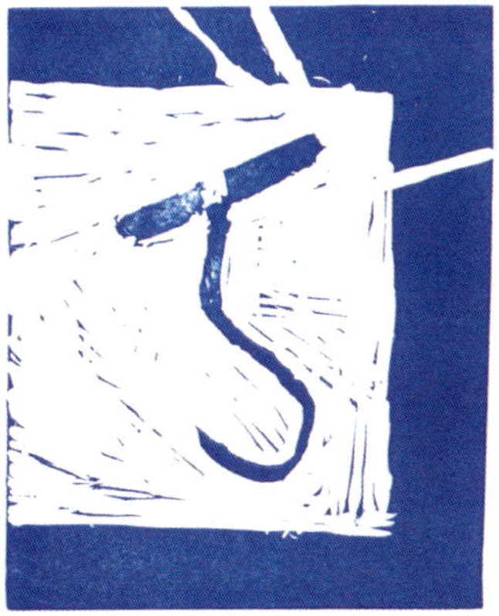
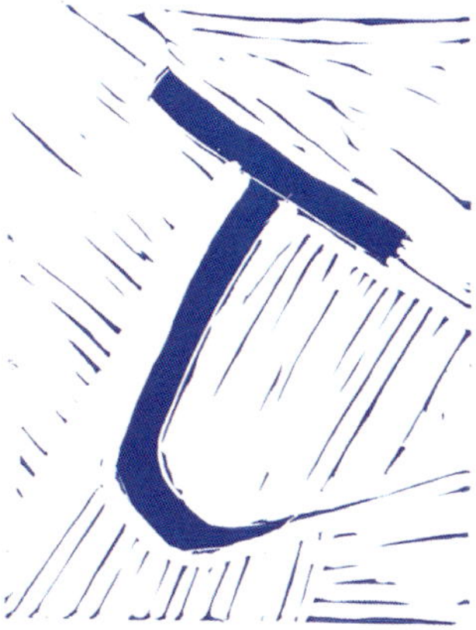

FIRST DAYS

At one workshop, the dockers were asked to recall their first day working on the docks. Most of the following stories were written by the dockers themselves, though a few were shared orally and transcribed by Fighting Words volunteers.

PADDY DALY

The first part of the day is easy enough to explain. There was a sense of awe and wonder, even dread, as you walked through the extension gates at North Wall, and you experienced for the first time, the din, the hustle and bustle of almost a thousand men, all packed together in a confined area. The billowing of cigarette smoke rising above the heads of the throng was so dense from a distance it gave the impression of a major fire.

Ideally, on your first day it was better to have someone with you that knew the ropes and procedure. At least to tell you where to go and what to listen for. As you are there for the first time in the read, with your deceased father's button displayed in the lapel of your jacket, you listen very carefully for the magic words, 'Any more button men?' You must now follow the lead of the men that have been picked before you and go to the foot of the picking out stand, and like them, hand in your cards to the company clerk that is standing there for that purpose. You must then, together with the rest of the men, await instructions from the foreman on where you should go. If you are totally ignorant of the geography of the place, then it's best to just follow the men that have been picked with you as part of a gang of men for a particular ship. On your way to the ship, get your social skills to kick in. Chat to one of the more friendly men in the gang. Tell him it's your first time, and hope that he takes pity on you.

image opposite

Dockers look for work at a 'Read' in North Wall

To be fair to them, the dockers were always very good, and very helpful to anybody just starting. It was a good idea on your first day to find out which men were friends with your father. That always helped.

When I finally arrived at my first ship, it was a small ship with a full cargo of grapes from Spain. The man I was working with called out to the singer-out for a tray (that is a pallet type – wooden platform with ropes attached). He showed me how to load the tray and the correct way to hook the tray onto the crane. After about five or six hoists, I started to get a bit of confidence and managed to get through the rest of the day with no problems. The ship finished at 4:00pm and we all returned to the shipping office, had our cards returned, and were paid for the day. I'm not sure what the money was, but I think it was thirty-six shillings.

Next morning, I stood in the read again, waited for 'any more button men' and went through the whole process again. This time, however, the cargo was timber and I was back to day one again. The gear for slinging timber was ropes – 'timber straps' to be exact. The lads I was working with showed me how to make a hoist of loose timber, using a timber strap. It didn't take too long until I started to get the hang of it. This ship finished at 6:30pm, and again I was given my cards and money. This time I was given the loose timber rate of thirty-nine shillings for the day, and two halves overtime.

Next morning, I went through it all again at the read, and back to day one again at the ship, because the cargo on this ship was barrels, and the lads had to show me how to use barrel hooks. The bottom line was that it took me eight to nine days, or should I say first days, before I got back to working a cargo that I had worked before… A young man starting on the docks, unlike his counterpart in industry, can experience as many as nine to ten first days.

It is difficult to describe how you felt on your first day. Me, personally, I felt it was a mixture of feelings; excitement on the one hand, and yet a sense of guilt on the other. Having priority of employment over older men in the read that had worked on the docks for many years before I arrived there at sixteen years of age. Many of these men had worked on the docks for far longer than that, yet now they had to concede to my priority through the power of a steel badge (the button) which I was wearing on the left lapel of my jacket. I was often asked how that made me feel. Well, maybe it was because of your age, but wearing the button on your jacket, you almost felt like the sheriff or deputy in a Western movie. You would have to remember the time we are talking about. They were very hard times. Work was scarce and wages were very low. Many of my contemporaries that I had went to school with could be employed as a messenger boy for a few quid a week, and but for the grace of God and the death of my father, I would very likely be doing the same. Having my father's button made it possible for me to earn more in one day than these lads would earn in a week. Because of your age and the fact that you were earning so much more money than your friends, there was a very real danger of becoming arrogant/conceited, resulting with you losing many of your best friends, and there were cases of that happening. I believe that respect was the key. Whether that was to your friends or the older generation of dockers, especially the non-button men. Respect seemed to transcend all other obstacles.

The upside of having a button (apart from the obvious), particularly if you were a member of a large family was that you could make life a lot better for them, and you gained so much respect from your siblings as a result. This made you feel good about yourself, and I believe it made you a better person in the process.

In Summary: For the non-button man, the button could be so unfair and made these men feel angry, even bitter. For those that were lucky enough to have a button, it was a God send. For me, it made me feel very much more secure than I would have been without it. I felt so fortunate to have had a button and it really did make a huge difference to my life. How would I have felt about working on the docks without a button? I simply don't know.

JOHN 'MILEY' WALSH

My first day on Dublin docks: I was only sixteen years old and totally ill-prepared for the environment I was walking into. I knew from my uncles a little about the read system, whereby I had to wait until the foreman shouted out 'any more button men?' That would be my signal to hand in my cards to the company clerk and begin my first day as a deep-sea docker.

Willie Downey had picked out for a boat with 1,000 tons of bags of cattle feed to go on transport to Paul & Vincents. He sent the first gang to No. 3 hatch, the second gang to No. 2 hatch, and we were off. Except for me. I stood around while everyone seemed to disappear in seconds. Luckily, I spotted a guy who had been called out immediately after me. He was the first non-button man picked out that day.

I decided if I was going to find out where this ship was berthed, I should follow this man. Off I went in pursuit, over to the step at the riverside to the Liffey Ferry, and I got a little worried when everyone but him and me got off, but I hadn't recognised any of them so I stuck with the one I did recognise. He carried on walking into a block of flats in Ringsend, then he discovered me and shouted down to me,

'Have you been following me?'

I shouted back, 'yes.' I explained that it was my first day and my first job. After a good laugh and several threats to tell the whole world, he asked if I had a bag hook[4]. I didn't even know what a bag hook was.

That man's name was Louis Reynolds, and he paired up with me inside that ship that day, and he educated me all that day and the next. I can still remember his attention to little details, and being clever about the way you work bags. He could have chosen another man to work with, but instead he looked after me when I needed it most. I and all the other guys like me found this attitude to be the norm. You got short and sharp lessons in how to do your work, and it was up to you if you did it the easy way or the hard way.

RICHARD 'BOXER' ELLIOT

It's 7:00 am.

My mother is pulling at my feet. 'Get up Dick. It's seven. Your Dad is sitting at the table. Hurry up and get that into you. The bus will be here at 7:30.'

'You will be standing in the read for George Bell. Willie Downey has an "Everard".'

'Just finished, Da.'

'Have you two got everything?'

'Yes, Ma.'

The bus is coming. We are on the bus.

'Hi Boxer[5], is he starting?'

'Yes.'

We reach the North Wall gates at the Point. Just inside the gate was the workplace in which all men gathered waiting for the read to start. The sound of everyone talking was deafening. The clock struck eight and everybody moved at the one time.

Me and my Dad shifted sideways like a crab. Willie Downey is doing the read, picking out the men. The first ship is a 'Yank'. My Dad gets a call for the 'Yank'. Four gangs of men go to the 'Yank' – all button men.

[4] *Hook with multiple prongs which was specifically designed for even distribution*

[5] *Richard's father was also nicknamed Boxer*

Next, my father is standing behind me. Willie Downey sees what is going on. He calls 'Boxer.' This read is for the 'Everard'. 'Go ahead son,' my Dad says, and I walk out and give my cards to the staff member who takes my cards and I am employed on the 'Everard'. On the way to the ship my Dad tells the men that got employed on it to look after me, and they did. They took me in hand and showed me how to make a hoist.

For the first couple of hours, I found it awkward. I was between 16 and 17 years of age. I was a quick learner – young and fit, but no experience. The man I am made up with is a neighbour. He took me in hand and I sailed through the job. That was 1962-63.

MICK FORAN

It was 1965, a miserable November morning. I was sixteen years of age, and it was my first day at Heiton's coal yard on Townsend Street. My older brother had gotten me a job there. On arrival, I was sent to work with a driver called Sean Redmond, nicknamed 'Kill the Cow'* to go with him to a five ton truck. We drive to the Custom House docks coal yard, and load seven tons of Polish coal packed in ten stone bags. The bags are filled by the machines and then loaded onto the truck by hand; I do this on my own while the driver goes to the canteen. I would get to go to the canteen if the truck was loaded before 10:00 am and would get a cup of tea with the driver in a broken cup or a jam jar.

Our delivery route for that day is for deliveries to the Georgian houses on Merrion Square, so we ask for an extra man because for these houses we had to carry bags of coal to the chambermaid's quarters at the top of the private houses. We go back to the yard for a second load at 1:00 pm. No lunch because I didn't know to bring one. We load the truck a second time. The same story for the afternoon, and we get back to Heiton's with the truck about 7:00 pm.

*'Kill the Cow' got his nickname because on a delivery to the Naas Road one day, he killed a cow on the back road and wrote off the truck. The farmer claimed for his dead cow but Heiton's countersued, won the case, and the farmer had to pay for the truck.

'A UNION JOB'
by Kay Foran

I was fifteen and working in a sewing factory in 1965 and didn't like it much; wages were lousy and conditions poor. I was giving out to my Da one day about the factory and he said, 'go get a union job, go down to Liberty Hall see a Mr. Duff on the sixth floor, tell him you're looking for work and I sent you down.'

The following day my friend Marie and I went as told; the receptionist eyed us up suspiciously when we asked to see Mr. Duff. 'What's it in connection with please?' she asked, looking at our mini skirts and beehives.

'Tell him Mr. Dunne sent us and it's about a job,' I answered. She glanced at the doorman and he grinned at us cheeky city kids.

She returned minutes later and let us up to the sixth floor. This was the first skyscraper we'd been in, and our maiden voyage in a lift, looking out over the city from Liberty Hall – this was the business! Mr. Duff sat behind a huge mahogany desk with a look of bafflement.

'My Da, Sean Dunne, sent us down. This is my friend Marie. We always work together, and we're looking for a union job.'

He smiled at his secretary and asked our ages and what kind of work we'd like. 'We don't like the sewing factories anymore, we like packing though,' Marie muttered. He replied scribbling 'There's a vacancy in Dublin Port Milling Company on Alexander Road, but it's for two lads!'

I replied, 'We can do the same as young fellas, and my Da works down the docks, and I know the area well!' (This was a blatant lie as we girls were never allowed go near the docks ever – it was a man's world down there in those times, with few women employed.)

He handed me a piece of paper. 'Give this to Paddy Murphy, you'll have to convince him yourself that yous can do the same work as the fellas. Good luck girls, it was lovely meeting yous.' We giggled as we left, and gave the receptionist a cheeky smirk as we exited the huge glass doors.

I couldn't wait for my Da to come home that evening. 'We have an interview on Alexander Road,' I said proudly.

'What? There's no way you're going down there. It's too dangerous for young ones down the docks,' he shouted at me.

'But you sent me to Mr. Duff yourself so we're going down tomorrow, I have the boss's name.' I ran into my bedroom, slamming the door.

I heard my Mam and Da muttering in the kitchen later that night. Before I went to bed my Da said, 'Make sure you get the early bus outside Geraghty butcher shop on Malborough Street. Don't be surprised if the fella runs the pair of ye, there's no one your age in the mill down there as far as I know.'

Next morning I heard my Da leave early for the docks on his bike. I called for Marie and we headed for the bus excitedly in the dark. There was a crowd of dockers smoking and chatting at the bus stop and I recognised some of my Da's mates. They were astonished to see us get on with them.

'That's Fatser's young one – don't take fare off them, I'll pay,' Pa Fagan said to the conductor. We were chuffed; that meant sixpence each for ourselves! (Pa was my Da's friend.)

The bus filled with smoke as the dockers puffed away, chatting and greeting each other. On our journey down through the city streets, they pointed out different factories and ships, and landmarks to us like we were tourists!

We got to the gate of Alexander Road and were amazed to see uniformed men manning the entrance to the port. 'They're okay,' Pa reassured us, 'they're Custom's Men or Harbour Police. You'll get used to them, Kay. If yous get the job they'll recognise you everyday.'

Dublin Port Milling Company was a huge site, full of trucks, silos, and forklifts, and huge weighing scales all over the yards, with loads of men in tan overalls driving and calling out to each other. Paddy Murphy's office was pointed out to us through the noise, and we were stared at by all as we crossed the yard. The smell was new to us – wheat, diesel, and fresh bread aroma distracted us as we filed into the offices.

Paddy Murphy was about six foot four, and didn't look remotely interested in speaking to us girls!

'Mr. Duff sent us from the Union, he said you're looking for two workers,' I said handing him the note.

'I am' he said, 'but not yous, I want two young fellas, this is dirty work and there's no girls could do it.'

'Well he sent us all the way down here. We can do packing or anything else like fellas.'

His face reddened and I thought he was gonna run us out.

'There's a packer needed in Procea Bakery here, but I need a fella for cleaning the Silo floor. There's huge machines there, it's not for girls!'

'Marie can pack. I'm a great cleaner at home, I'd like the Silo,' I volunteered cheekily.

'You can't wear mini skirts up there, you'd need jeans and overalls,' he replied just as cheekily. We stood our ground silently, staring ahead.

'Okay!' He said at last, 'I'll try yous out. Weekly wages is six pounds ten shilling,' I nearly choked, we'd been getting two pounds ten shillings in the sewing factory – this was nearly three times that much.

'Start next Monday, get a docket on your way out for overalls in O'Connors on Abbey street. Don't come back without jeans or yous can't start, is that clear?' He slammed the office door and left us grinning at each other 'Jesus Kay, six ten! Wait till we tell your Da.' We went home on an empty bus, chatting excitedly to the conductor, telling him the news about our good fortune.

We sauntered up town on Saturday to O'Connors for our overalls. The docket was for ten pounds each. Jeans were only coming out in Dublin and we were thrilled to be able to buy two pairs each of the latest Wrangler jeans and two lovely pink nylon overalls – we'd be in the height of fashion going to work. We danced around proudly that night in the Galway Arms, showing off our Wranglers to our mates.

Monday came and I loved the job immediately. I left so confident in my lovely gear. Paddy sent Marie to the Bakery, but escorted me personally up to the first floor of the gigantic silo. The sound was deafening; huge machines roared and spun leather belts through each floor. Paddy introduced me to Christy, a big man with a huge belly in his boiler suit, he had a lovely round smiling face with friendly eyes.

'I'll watch her Paddy, she'll be grand.' He smiled at me and handed me a huge, wide yard brush. Paddy left, relieved. I got the feeling that Paddy didn't like girls much.

'Keep your eye on that machine Kay, and if the floor overflows, sweep it aside and put it over there in the bin. Careful now, never go too near the belts or you'll be sucked in and we'll never see you again.' He patted my shoulder, 'Keep your eye out for Paddy, he's always on the prowl. He's not the worst, he's shy around the women though.' We chatted about families and where we each lived and in no time at all Christy sent me off for tea break. 'Come back in a half hour Kay,' he said, pointing to a large building across the yard.

The canteen was large and clean and smelled of home. Women and men were in separate rooms; in the middle was a huge serving area where a lovely lady, Evelyn, served all with freshly fried breakfasts or lovely sandwiches. Formica tables and chairs were filled by women in different coloured overalls, some wearing turbans on their heads. Marie and I were made welcome, and shown around the dressing rooms and toilets, and were amazed to see two fold away beds. 'For when you're not feeling so well,' Evelyn said smiling.

There was a machine like a telescope in the bathroom, girls chatted and washed their hands. One walked over put her hands into the head of the machine. 'That's a Handy Andy girls, for drying your hands.' Imagine a hand dryer, this was like America! We were so excited. About twenty women in all worked in the different parts of the mill. All were older, some as old as forty, but mostly girls in their twenties.

The Mill was such an education for us, the perks of a union job impressed us, work hours were regular, food was supplied for fair money weekly. We got used to paying Union dues weekly – a first for us then.

We loved the glamour of the job. We finished early afternoon each Friday and most of the girls got ready in work for their Friday Nights out in the City's Ballrooms like Clery's. The Metropol and the Crystal were all new to us, we were too young for them. We went to the Galway Arms, the Matt Talbot, or the Go Go in Sackville Place, across from Clery's Ballroom.

The girls showered, did each other's hair, makeup, nails, and swapped clothes for their dances every Friday evening. Most lived in Ringsend or Pearse Street or Irishtown and crossed the ferry daily to and from work. Imagine the glamour – we'd never been on a ferry.

I loved Mondays break time when we'd listen wide eyed to their tales of the weekend's Ladies' Choices, jiving competitions, their favourite bands and singers like Frankie McBride and the Polka Dots, Earl Gill. We were more into Mod music. The Beatles had arrived, and Marie loved the Rolling Stones. We were miles apart musically, but swapped the gossip and records happily with our older work mates.

I got used to the hard work on the silos, but the men always gave me a hand. They carried heavy buckets of water. I was like the protected species most times. I'd listen to their stories of kids, football, dart matches, pool halls, and Christy introduced me to the crosswords in the daily newspaper, which I still enjoy fifty years later.

It was such an exciting and educational time and in the summer we enjoyed walking around the docks, watching my father and his friends unload timber and coal boats. We felt safe always amid the hustle and bustle of the busy dockside and factories. Also, in the summer we'd have weekend excursions and dinner dances to Wicklow, Arklow, and Bray. We'd head off in our finery, singing happily on the buses, with money to spend among trusted and respected work mates. They minded us well and we were always escorted home safely to our front doors, having drank one Babycham each, feeling glamourous and grown up.

I stayed on for over two years and left the Mill at eighteen to marry a docker's son and we headed to Birmingham – but that's another story!

DECLAN BYRNE

I started as a junior clerk in Dublin docks in 1973, at the age of eighteen. In dockland terms, I would have been considered as 'half a gobshite' – foolish, but not deserving of the full title. Added to my lack of cop-on was my overriding desire to be popular and to be accepted. This combination was to lead me into many a tight corner. My Dad, Martin, had a saying (in actual fact he had hundreds of sayings, some of which were in total contradiction, such as 'the man who made time made plenty of time' and 'time and tide waits for no man.') In this case I am referring to 'it is better to be born lucky than cute' and as life has progressed I have depended time after time on my good luck.

In 1973, I lived in Ballybough on Orchard Road. For me, working on the docks was like entering an alien planet. I found myself working with dockers and checkers, some of whom could trace their family involvement in the docks back five and in some cases six generations. My Dad was a builder's labourer hailing from Wicklow, while my Mam was from North Strand. I was assigned to the wages office with Pat Walsh and Joe Keenan. It was an exceptionally busy office. Using checkers dockets I had to calculate the dockers' daily pay. Each day the dockers would come to the hatch to check their previous day's pay, and it was then that I was introduced to the banter. I also had to pay a gratuity to crane men who were not employees, but were paid a top up for a job well done. The auditor insisted that they sign a docket each time I paid them, but he wasn't amused when the majority of them signed as Mickey Mouse or Donald Duck.

JIMMY PURDY

I left school at fourteen to take up a job as a messenger boy in Hunt Bros Provisions on Grand Canal Street. The next year I started a new job as a lift operator in the Friends Provident on Dame Street. The building is still there with the famous 'Pen Corner' on the ground floor. The lift was manually operated and I had to control the speed and make sure we stopped in the right position on each floor, based on the amount of people on board which affected the total weight in the lift.

When I was sixteen I got an interview with the Dublin Port and Docks along with six other boys. We were interviewed by Mr. Buckley in a large office with him sitting behind a big mahogany desk. All the other boys were sons of tradesmen and they all got apprenticeships to the various trades their fathers belonged to. My father Richard worked in the port but was not a tradesman. He had gotten work in the port because he had served in the Royal Navy during the first world war. He lied on his application and joined the Navy when he was fifteen saying he was eighteen. We still have the log of his service record.

I got a job as a nipper. The job of a nipper was to run errands and make tea for the other workers. I started work at 8:15 am, later than the older guys. We were building the ship berth where the current Stena Line operates from. When I arrived at work in the morning, the fire was already lit and it was my job to keep the fire going and the water boiling for making tea at 10:00 am for morning tea break, dinner time at 1:00 pm, as it was called then, and afternoon tea at 3:30 pm. Between that and running for messages to the shops on East Wall Road for all the senior workers, mostly for cigarettes and tobacco, I was kept busy all day.

One of my fondest memories is of how I managed the fire. I would be given a bag of coal on a Monday morning, delivered by the coalman on a horse and cart from the main yard on East Wall Road. This was supposed to last all week, but the coal was always gone on Tuesday morning when I came in to work because each of the guys would take just a little bit. For three years I would go down to the basin when the tide went out and collect driftwood and lay it out to dry. This allowed me to keep the fire going all week so there was never an issue about the missing coal. The men I worked with were a lovely group all from the city centre, and they showed their appreciation by making a collection every Friday and gave me enough money to buy my first bike, by the week, in Paddy Whelan's in Cork Street. It was a semi sports bike, with straight handlebars instead of dropped handlebars and three speed Sturmey-Archer gears.

AN Average Day

During one workshop at Fighting Words, the dockers were asked to describe their average day on the docks, or a memory from about ten years into working on the docks.

JOHN 'MILEY' WALSH

After several years, I got the hang of most of the hard jobs. The trick was if you couldn't avoid it, you'd better get stuck in and move on. In 1971, decasualisation came not overnight, but after years of tough negotiation. This was the first time that the deep-sea dockers were paid any kind of a regular week's wage. A wage was made up of whatever work you did at a ship, and if no ships were in port you would get a payment called fall back pay. This was by no means sufficient to get you a mortgage, but it was preferable to going to the labour.[6]

The system of employment changed. No more looking up at the faces of the foreman and living in hope. Now everything was done in alphabetical order or numerical order. It ensured that brothers, cousins, and namesakes all began working together, and it remains to be seen if this was a better system.

The biggest change that came at this time was the shift to palletised cargos and the introduction of containers. A new company arrived to take over all stevedoring owned in total by Dublin Port and Docks Board. I suspect they moved in on the other companies because of a lack of investment by the stevedores who built facilities in other ports; like George Bell, who took all their work to Rosslare where they built a new container handling facility and moved out of Dublin never having owned a crane or even a forklift truck.

Dublin Maritime was another company who re-invested its profits outside Dublin. They set up a new facility in Waterford, taking work out of Dublin. So it came to pass that all deep-sea dockers were now in the employ of a company called Dublin Cargo Handling, one-hundred percent owned by the port board. Things changed drastically then. This company took health and safety seriously, and we began a system of training for each and every man who had an interest in driving equipment such as forklifts, two tons to forty tons, bobcats, mechanical diggers, and cranes.

image opposite
'Standing in for loose' outside the gates of the North Wall

[6]
Having to claim social welfare payments

The next move for me was to do a course in training all dockers of all jobs described. I became assistant to the training instructor, but I was left to do most of it myself as the instructor was also a foreman and was hardly available. We set up training courses, which turned into competition courses with lots of winner's prizes, cash and other stuff. We had winners in the All Ireland competitions as well, so our training was paying dividends.

To sum up my entire working life on the docks, it has to be said it was by any man's standards a fantastic job to work in. Every single day brought you a different experience; it was like working in a different job every day of your life. In my forty-six years, I experienced the highs and the lows a person would get from any job, but with that I got the almost military standard backing when things went awry.

Looking back now, I don't think we really understood what we had and if I could turn the clock back I would be rewinding straight away. Would I do anything different?

I don't think so.

DECLAN BYRNE

Ten years later, I was still a junior clerk working in the North Wall extension under two dock superintendents, Liam Warren and Karl Keaveney, referred to as Mr. Tayto, having previously been a boss at Tayto. Karl Keaveney was an absolute gentlemen to work for and I could fill a book with his stories and incidents that occured when I worked there. It was frowned upon if an office member joined a union. I was advised by a fellow office staff member to become a 'secret' member of the Federated Workers Union of Ireland. I did this for a while but it seemed pointless to pay money and not be officially represented. So I decided to join the Marine Port and General Workers' Union, which was was deemed as an act of treason. Captain Burke told me that as long as I remained in the Dublin docks even to the age of sixty-five, I would remain as a junior clerk. Some predictions in life turn out to be true.

RICHARD 'BOXER' ELLIOT

I am now working for Dublin Maritime Shipping driving a forklift. Newsprint paper always came on the roll in the hold of a ship. The men in the hatch would take wedges from under the reel of paper and prize it out with a special type of stick that fits into the tiny gap in the reel. As the bottom reel came out, the two top ones would roll with it, then I would put a sling around it and send three or four reels out to the men on the wall.

One day Mr. Newman came to me and said, 'Get in the car.'

'What the fuck is going on?'

'Get in the car. We are just going around to No. 6 shed. I am going to show you how to use a clamp on your fork.'

'Okay,'

When I got to No. 6, the fork and clamp were waiting for me. I had to learn how to use the clamp so I could stand the paper on end. So I played with it for a couple of days. By the end of that week, we had a ship from Canada with paper newsprint. Standing on its end! Never before did newsprint come in a ship standing on its end, and never before was paper tiered on its end in the shed. So me and Valley Fulham had to try and show the fork drivers that were sent over to the ship. All we could do is just show them the basic way to do it. Just show them how it works, the rest is up to them. And this is on the day of the ship.

Well, I needn't tell you some of the drivers were insurance nightmares. The paper was left in shreds. Some of the rolls were that bad that you couldn't get a piece big enough to wipe your ass!

So Valley and I had to drive, him in one gang and me in the other. Eventually, some of the drivers began to get it and all was well. The ship was a great job. She would work Friday to Saturday to Sunday. A very well paying job.

JIMMY PURDY

As I came up to twenty-one, I had to train in a new boy to take over my 'nipper' job, his name is Philip Lynch and we still meet to this day.

Once he was trained in, I got the job of looking after the Customs Officers' offices around the port. There were four of them, one at Spencer Dock, one at the Custom House, one at Alexander Basin, and one on the southside, close to Pearse Street. I would clock in at East Wall and clock out on the southside at 5:15 p.m. because it was close to home. My job was to keep everything clean and tidy in each of the offices.

I then worked as a labourer on the building site that was constructing the first Ro-Ro (Roll on Roll Off) berth in the port. It was not put into use until the late seventies due to union opposition. This was all on reclaimed land, and the project was managed by 'The Dutchman' who was probably 'Dutch' because of their expertise at land reclamation.

When I was twenty-three, my wife Bernie was having our first baby, who had a small problem and they were transferred to James' Street Maternity for two weeks. During that two weeks I was made redundant because of cutbacks from the new government of 1956.

When I told Bernie, she said 'that's great, you can help me with the baby.' We were living with her father, Charlie Downey, who was active in the War of Independence and became a Captain in the Army, serving as the Governor of a jail in Kerry and at Portlaoise. When he left the army, he became a button man.

When he would have a few drinks on him he would go on and on about his exploits in the War of Independence, but he was a good guy and after two years on the labour he got me a job in Dunlop's. I worked there from 1958 to 1984 when they closed down and I was made redundant again. From 1984 to 1996, when I retired, I worked as a security man in Belvedere College.

image opposite
Discharging steel bars on the quay side

STORY TELLERS

The following are stories that the dockers found particularly amusing or interesting. Fighting Words cannot guarantee that every piece that follows is totally factual and free of exaggeration, although we can guarantee that they will be entertaining.

RICHARD 'BOXER' ELLIOT

Coming to the end of the day at around 7:30pm, Goldfinger appears out of nowhere after being missing all day. The foreman, Mumper, spots Goldfinger walking through the gate.

'You're sacked.'

Goldfinger whispers something in Mumper's ear. Next all hell breaks loose.

Mumper says, 'I don't give a bollocks. You are sacked.'

Then Goldfinger says, 'Then what have I to do? A month in prison like you did?' Mumper went to kill Goldfinger. The argument went on until the ship knocked off at 7:45pm.

I walked home with Goldfinger. 'What was all that about?'

'I just told him that I had to meet my mot[7] and give her her money.' Now that might be true, but eight hours to give her money is a bit thick. That was on the first day of the ship. So Goldfinger was sacked until the ship was finished.

[7] *Wife or partner*

FROM THE SESSIONS

'From the time I was a kid, the docks on the northside of the quays was my playground. There was the Guinness barges that would drop their cargo of barrels like wooden kegs. Me and my friends would run along the top of the barrels. Moving down to the "B&I" and "The Kilkenny," hooshing the cattle across the road.'

'The read for the ship was 8:00 am Monday morning. The six men inside the ship, and one singer out. Outside the ship there were nine men on three trucks – three on each truck. On my truck was Harry Lennon, Paddy Burke, and myself. The three of us got together as we were picked in the read. As for the other six, they paired off on the way over to the ship. On the second truck there was 'Pa' Fagan, Bernard McCluskey, and 'Fatser' Dunne. On the third truck was Ben Hannigan, Larry Corbally, and Lawlor. I never knew Lawlor's first name as long as I knew him, but as for the other seven we all lived a stone's throw from each other. Lawlor lived in Ballyfermot. Ben and Larro dived on Lawlor to work on their truck. You see, Ben and Larro were playing League of Ireland football at this time and they were looking for a gillie so they could go to training for their game on Sunday. So when they picked up their truck in the gear-shed they were rubbing their hands. After finding their bearings, and taking their first hoist over to the 'tier' and after unloading the truck, they said to Lawlor 'you go home now, and me and Larro will take our time off later. So you go on we will see you tomorrow morning.' That is when all the fun started. The ship worked up to 8:00 pm that night Ben and Larro did a great job, they worked hard that day. The next morning: no sign of Lawlor. At 8:10 pm a young lad of about eleven was standing at the gangway looking for the foreman on the ship, when the foreman saw the young lad, he asked him 'who are you looking for?'

'A Mr. Flood.'

'That's me son, what can I do for you?'

'My Dad said I have to give you this.'

'And what is that?'

'A letter.'

The foreman was 'Bomber' Flood, a decent man. He read the letter.

'Okay son, you go home now and mind yourself on the way out of here. Here you two – Ben and Larro! That young lad was Lawlor's son. He's not able to come in today, he has a dose of the runs and you both are going to work it out for Lawlor.'

'Okay.'

'Okay.'

Ben: 'We are fucked. We won't be able to get an early dinner never mind go training.'

Larro: 'He better be in, in the morning.'

The other trucks could come and go as they wished, it was bell to bell for Ben and Larro. If Paddy or Harry wanted to do or go somewhere, there was no bother. The same with the other truck.

Day three, and no sign of Lawlor. Ben and Larro are stripping their truck. 'The Tierer' John Roe starts to take the piss out of Ben and Larro.

'That sham Lawlor, there is fucking nothing wrong with him, I saw him walking past Clery's, his mot was behind him with a poe.'

Ben said, 'would you ever fuck off.'

Larro: 'That cunt better be here in the morning, I don't give a fuck about 'Bomber.' He can go fuck himself, I have a pain in my bollix working for that cunt. I'm on my hands and knees.'

Ben: 'We won't be able to kick a ball, never mind run after one on Sunday.'

JOHN 'MILEY' WALSH

Back in the early '70s we worked quite a lot of West African ships. They carried everything from cocoa beans and timber to containers. The timber was mostly all hardwood, like mahogany, teak, black ebony – all really heavy timber where we could earn a good day's pay through our bonus scheme.

I remember one particular ship that arrived late one day, and they employed three gangs to work her. The deck of No. 4 hatch was loaded with about fifty empty 20 ft containers and we had to discharge them before we could get opened up to get at the timber and earn a good day's pay. That day I was employed as a winch driver. These ships carried single derrick winches at both ends of the hatch and could lift 25 tons in heavy gear, but we were in a hurry so we used the light gear to speed things up.

The gang that day were a pleasure to work with. They were one of the best gangs you could ever have and you needed to be on your game to keep up with them. Their name was Caulfield, from Ringsend – several brothers and all business.

The gang decided to forget about the container spreader, as you could only get one container at a time. Instead they used a double set of chains to hook on two containers at a time. They even tried four on one occasion, until the foreman came along screaming. No matter, they grabbed at the the hooks each time I came over the hatch.

When a gang was working like that everyone has to watch after everyone else. You have eyes for nothing else. So it was then that I became oblivious to what was going on on the lower deck. Someone said to me, 'watch the crew, they're all gathering in a very dangerous spot near you.'

Suddenly I realised what I had been screaming every time I slewed in over the containers: 'OVER YOUR HEAD SAMBO!' It hit me like a brick. I had to get the foreman to explain to the chief officer that one of our dockers was called Sambo.

I stayed at the winch that day a little longer than I had intended and, lucky for me, when I apologised to the bosun[8] later that day, they saw the funny side of it and even supplied me with refreshing cold Harp Lager. All's well that ends well.

'FROM THE DOCKS TO BURMA AND HOME AGAIN'
by Bernard 'Barney' O'Connor

[8] *A ship's officer in charge of equipment and the crew*

Barney was just fifteen when he finished school and started working on the docks in the winter of 1943. He remembers it was a cold winter, one where there was no canteen near. He kept a flask with him, and stayed warm by wrapping up in a pre-worn overcoat. If he got too hot while working, he would roll the sleeves up.

Barney is the eldest son of Bernard Senior, a shed man who worked for the Limerick Steam Ship Company. Barney's father would locate items in the sheds for customs spot checks. That winter they needed extra help, and so Barney joined his father and began a lifelong adventure at the mouth of Dublin Bay.

Brandy features in one of Barney's earliest memories from the docks. He would work all day putting 'scorchers' under the barrels (to stop them from rolling) and then, in turn, banging the bung up out of each barrel. An officer came along with a dipstick to measure the brandy, and he would also take a sample from each barrel. Once collected, the samples went through a lengthy process in the state laboratory in Dublin Castle, taking as long as three months to clear.

'We worked with the Goodwin brothers and the Gorman brothers,' Barney recalls. 'It was a real family affair' with the two sets of brothers and a father and son.

The work was on and off, and Barney hoped for something more permanent. He remembers there being 'very little work then. Very little coming and very little going out. And there was ration cards then: food, clothing.' Within the year, he saw an ad in *The News of the World*; the British government were looking for recruits for the army and the Air Force.

Having always wanted to fly, Barney took the train to Belfast and went to Anne Street, where the recruiting office was located. He had to pay his own fare.

Just a week later, he was on his way back to Belfast; this time, the fare was paid for by his new employer. From there, he went straight on to Regent Street in London for medical tests, then Cranwell for his training. Barney went from being a docker to flying in just a matter of weeks.

The Air Force wasn't all glamour; Barney recalls that the airplanes 'were very ancient planes. They were called 'Miles Majesters'. They used to say that Miles Majesters were around when Pontius was a pilot.'

While in the Air Force, Barney travelled to Burma, what is now Myanmar. There was only one time Barney recalled feeling homesick while in Rangoon: 'There was a church, a huge church, the whole side was blown out and covers were attached. I said to the guy, "what do you have?" and he said that they always have the same thing: egg, steak and chips, or chicken and chips. Now you never saw a chicken in the whole of India or Burma in your life. But something was better than rations. So we decided to have chicken and chips. It was black. I said to the guy, "have you got any liquer?" and he said "yeah, whiskey." They could produce stuff from nowhere. He put a bottle down and I poured a glass, and the next thing I know I saw a shadow in front of me. I looked up and there was a woman officer. "You're too young to be drinking that." So I looked up, and I was a bit of a smart Alec, a bit cheeky, so I looked up and said to her "I may be a bit young to drink that but I'm not too young to come out here and get bloody killed am I?" She said "oh, cheeky as usual." She was a neighbour: Mary Mullaney.' Despite being over 5,000 miles away from home, the two Dubliners each found a familiar face.

Four and a half years later, Barney came home. He worked for a few months in Dublin Airport training pilots for Aer Lingus' new transatlantic routes which were being introduced. A change in government brought this opportunity to an end, and Barney returned to the docks.

He was employed as a checker on his return, and aged just twenty-three, he found himself his own father's boss.

Barney kept up his education during his time in the Air Force, and when he returned the Air Force then paid for him to attend Trinity College – an opportunity he happily took. Barney believed that his education helped him to handle the men and the responsibility better.

He went on to do a Masters and then 'got a bit cocky.' During his primary degree, Barney would do half of his college work in the mornings, and then the other half at night so that it fit around his work schedule. He studied Irish history, and his Masters was in the same subject. Barney also did a PhD in the Free University of Ireland 20 years after he retired. He began lecturing when he was 65 years old. He continued lecturing until his wife became ill.

Barney is 94 now, and attended his granddaughter's graduation recently.

DECLAN BYRNE

I found myself working in the deep-sea section of the docks, where ninety-nine percent of the workers were drawn from the close-knit communities of Ringsend, Pearse Street, City Quay, East Wall, North Wall, and the North Inner City. In good times they had a tendency to fight like cats and dogs and in times of hardship the solidarity was truly unbelievable. It would take a book to describe the hard times and the acts of generosity that I witnessed, but for now I will satisfy myself with telling you about the morality of smuggling.

When word got out that I was working on the docks I received an unexpected knock on the door. A neighbour, around my own age, wanted me to smuggle a pair of motorbike boots for him. He informed me with some authority that all I needed to do was to go aboard a Polish vessel in the port and purchase said boots. So a few days later I left the office with my few bob to go aboard the Polish. Once aboard I met an obliging seaman who seemed to know what I was talking about. He led me down into the crew's quarters and gave me the pick of a number of boots. He told me to stuff them down the front of my trousers. I was never so well-endowed in all my life. Fastening my jacket, the job was 'oxo[9].' Well, it was until I went down the gangway. Two custom's cars came racing towards me as if they were on a drugs bust. I was informed of my rights and told to open my jacket. The docker foreman at the ship was Paddy Kelly (his Dad was Patsy Kelly and was known as 'Big Nose' which resulted in Paddy

[9] *The job's oxo is a Dublin phrase meaning a job has been completed*

being referred to as 'Little Big Nose.') I noticed that he was observing the proceedings from the deck of the ship. One particular customs officer was taking delight in my predicament. He told me I would be charged with smuggling, that the boots would be confiscated as evidence, that my employer would be immediately informed and that more than likely I would be sacked. 'Little Big Nose' roared over the side of the ship, 'Will you leave that young fella alone – can't you see he hasn't got an arse in his trousers. He started work last week and he can't afford the bus fare. He bought a motorbike and the gobshite hasn't got a helmet or boots!' This intervention of lies did the trick; they even handed the boots back to me with a warning that they wouldn't be as lenient if they caught me the next time.

That night I brought the boots up to Tolka Road and my "friend" didn't like the style of them. I felt like bouncing them off his head or at least off his front door but being of a windy disposition I retired, disgusted and out of pocket.

In my twenty-seven years working in Dublin docks I saw some great strokes (though the biggest strokes were always done by fellows in suits.) I also saw some smuggling.

Looking back now I can say that I nearly saw everything smuggled, with the exception of drugs. I knew early on that I was no master criminal, so I never opted for the smuggling career path. While I worked in the docks someone remarked that I was 'good with the pen' and that I should write down some of the dockland stories. Overhearing the conversation, Peter 'Blake' Montgomery said 'but Declan cannot swim.' As I still cannot swim, I am going to steer away from any reference to what I would consider commercial smuggling and concentrate on the more acceptable face of smuggling.

In my period on the docks I worked in the Ocean Pier, the North Wall Extension, and the South Bank Quay in Ringsend. The South Bank was referred to as 'Long Kesh' because if you were transferred there you had little chance of ever escaping. It was here that I worked with some very sound people, and it is here that my next smuggling story begins.

In other parts of the docks, different categories of staff were more separate. In the South Bank, we were more of a crew. There were fitters who maintained the side-loaders and the heavy forklifts; there were fitter's helpers: machine drivers, groupage men, checkers, clerks, and various other species. When you think of a fitter's helper you might be inclined to think of someone young, but one of them, Joe, was no spring chicken, but he was one of the soundest people I have ever worked with. Joe had his daughter's wedding coming up so he decided to smuggle in booze for the wedding (a totally acceptable practice as far as we were all concerned.) Yes, he was caught using a forklift and yes, there were over six cases of spirits on the pallet – but remember, it was for his daughter's wedding. The customs officer who made the capture, even before this, was affectionately known as the 'Red Louse.' Joe received a very hefty fine. His job was not threatened because of the unwritten rule: robbing is a sacking offence, smuggling is not. There was a wave of sympathy for Joe, and a wave of anger directed at the customs officer. On top of the expenses for the wedding, Joe now had a large fine to pay. A raffle was organised with tickets printed and most if not all the money was raised to pay the fine. The 'Red Louse' was about as popular as a fart in an astronaut's suit, and there were those who advocated retribution. Joe had to call a meeting in the staff canteen to ask people to take no action. The talk was of placing a container on his car or putting sugar in his petrol tank, but people agreed to abide by Joe's wishes. Over time, the incident began to fade from people's memories.

The South Bank had a permanent workforce which was supplemented by dockers who were allocated to work the various container vessels on a daily basis. On a sunny Saturday I saw a docker enter the compound. I knew him by name, but not personally. His nickname was 'Nudger' (even sometimes referred to as 'Big Nudger' even though he was small in stature.) What a great nickname to have! He called into the office and told me to watch him. It was a strange request because I knew that he didn't want me to stand nix. I was picked because I was in radio (walkie-talkie) contact with all the staff on the berth. I knew something unusual was going to happen and it was not long before I had a discreet crowd in attendance, all carefully hidden behind containers. The customs office was next to my office, and it contained a large window which gave them a good view of the terminal. I saw Nudger parade past the window more than once. From the distance, I could see that there was something down the front of Nudger's trousers. At South Bank it would not have been unusual for someone to smuggle a single bottle of vodka down the front of their trousers. The aforementioned customs officer appeared from the office calling on Nudger to halt. It was a hot day and the officer was not in full uniform (he was not wearing his jacket.) He announced that he was customs and that he intended on searching Nudger.

'You could be the man on the moon as far as I am concerned, and how do I know that you are customs?' asked Nudger. The officer raced into the office and returned in uniform. In the intervening period Nudger had made a token effort to exit the compound. The officer caught up with him and Nudger was quick to say, 'I know my rights – I am entitled to see your identification.' This necessitated another frantic back and forth race. The hidden crowd were starting to sense the excitement. Out of breath, he caught up with Nudger and placed his hand on his shoulder saying, 'I have reason to believe that you have smuggled spirits about your person.' In one perfect hand movement, Nudger produced a large bottle of Guinness from his jocks and and produced in his other hand a bottle opener, and in a matter of seconds he had the open bottle to his lips, declaring, 'I always like my Guinness at body temperature.'

This was greeted with ringing cheers from the now emerging crowds. 'You are a right bastard for doing this to me,' said the officer.

'Not as big a bollix as you were to Joe,' came the instant reply. This incident has now gone down in dockland folklore a bit like the General Post Office in 1916 – at least five hundred people claimed to have witnessed it. Nudger passed away a number of years ago, a well-known docker from Pearse Street, may he rest in peace (or knowing him, he is still getting up to devilment.) On that day, Nudger gave me a practical lesson in the value of nonviolent action. I salute all the planning and effort he put into the execution of the task. That afternoon is a standout memory of the twenty-seven years in Dublin docks. Nudger, like many other dockers was no angel, but he will always stand tall in my admiration. A beacon of a working class person teaching us how we should stick together and look after each other and 'fuck the begrudgers' (I am not sure if that's one of my Dad's sayings.)

image opposite

Meat getting ready for export outside the old Point Depot

DANGERS AND DEATHS

Although many Dublin dockers remember their time on the docks fondly, it was a very dangerous job. Men were crushed or hit by extremely heavy cargo; wires snapped and cranes bent. More than a few dockers drowned. Dockers were constantly at risk of either injury or death from physical trauma.

Dublin ambulances became known as 'the dockers' taxi.' In addition to injury, many dockers contracted diseases from working on the docks – diseases like Black Lung.

Black Lung (Coal Workers' Pneumoconiosis) is a disease caused by long periods of exposure to coal dust. When a person repeatedly inhales coal dust, the dust will coat the inside of their lungs and lead to respiratory issues. If a docker had gone to a doctor and described his symptoms, he simply would have been told to stop smoking. Many dockers who developed Black Lung died young and without a proper diagnosis.

Dockers were also in constant danger of inhaling asbestos. Some boats would carry bags that would disintegrate into fibers in the dockers hands. The fibers would fly out and cling to their clothes, and dockers would often unknowingly inhale them. These bags were most likely coated with friable (disintegrating) asbestos, which is the most dangerous kind. Dockers who regularly handled asbestos developed minor asbestosis at best, or at worst they developed lung cancer and mesothelioma. When Paddy Daly mentioned these 'flakes of blue and white dust' he saw to the Union, they ordered him to stay quiet. If he didn't, they said, Dublin dockers' work would be redirected to Belfast.

Some dockers' deaths were tragic because nothing could have been done to stop them; other deaths were tragic because they were so easily preventable. There was very little done to protect the dockers prior to 1989. The docks were often overlooked in Health and Safety Acts – both Irish and English. There were lax Health and Safety regulations introduced in the 70s and 80s, but ship captains could often be bribed to ignore those regulations for a bottle of whiskey.

The following chapter attempts to recount in the dockers' own words the dangers that they and their companions faced.

DECLAN BYRNE

I was lucky to have worked with James McKane. James started off as a seaman, and on shore he was a gearman. Later, the rules were bent and he became a docker. He died tragically in the hatch of a ship.

Dockers used to honour a deceased docker by carrying their coffin from some distance to the doors of the church, where the family would then take over. This tradition continued for many years on the Northside and the Southside of the Liffey. It now only continues in Ringsend thanks to the efforts of Boy Murphy and Lar Dunne.

In the case of James McKane, Danny Gahen stepped out in front, some distance from Our Lady of Victories Church on Ballymun Road, and nearly gave the hearse driver a heart attack. A particular docker who I had several run-ins with asked if I wanted to be the first to carry the coffin. Another docker overheard it and said 'no way is he a docker —' but the first one you didn't argue with, and it was the greatest honour of my life.

BRENDA[10]

[10] Name has been changed on request

Brenda came into the Dockers' Sessions in order to find more information on her father. Brenda's Dad worked with Morgan Mooney's. Morgan Mooney's was a fertiliser company, according to one of the deep-sea dockers present. Brenda doesn't know what her Dad worked as and is looking for any information relating to him or her grandfather who worked on the docks as a foreman. Brenda has only recently discovered where her Dad is buried, in Kinsealy. Brenda's Dad died at the age of 39 in 1949. He died of throat cancer, which was not stated on his death certificate. Brenda's mother was left a widow with 2 daughters. Brenda was six years old when he died, and has no memory of her father. Brenda remembers a happy childhood, skipping ropes in Croke Park near her home. Brenda is now living in Kilbarrack, having returned from London in 1972. Brenda was reared on the North Circular Road, then went to the UK where she stayed for thirteen years and later got married. Brenda has eight children, seventeen grandchildren, and thirteen great-grandchildren.

FROM THE SESSIONS

'Back then you had grain ships and coal ships, and phosphorite for fertiliser, and iron, timber, flour, fruit. Working in the hole you'd put a little pebble or a button or a little piece of coal in your mouth and keep it moist all the time. Now in my opinion, the hardest job was the copper ore, what you call iron ore. It was so hard to get through it with a shovel. It was so heavy. You used a number five shovel, a smaller one. That was, physically, the hardest job. And on top of that, you got acid from it. You could get acid into you and your teeth and tongue would go black. You'd come home and give the teeth the old brush. I used to use salt and soot.'

DANGERS AND DEATHS

'If you were called to do anything, you were able to do it – pulling a truck, tiering in sheds, slinging in the hole, driving a winch. And you took pride in doing it. But there was always danger working on the docks. I saw a man being killed with a tub of coal. He was a workmate. We were working the ship's gear and the wire broke on the winch and it just buried him in the coal. And I always felt that the long steel rails, thirty or forty foot long, was a very dangerous job. Always afraid of wires bursting if overweight when you were hoisting it. And it did happen.'

⇦ ⇨ ⇦ ⇨ ⇦ ⇨

'Snakes and spiders on those banana ships. Coming from Africa. They used to come in stalks and now they come in containers. But it was one bag in each hand on the back of your neck, and anything could fall onto the back of your shirt.'

⇦ ⇨ ⇦ ⇨ ⇦ ⇨

'When you lifted, you had to be very careful. The whole bottom of a bag would be eaten by rats. The bag wouldn't disintegrate. As you threw the bag over yourself, you'd have to keep your trousers tied because the rats would be running about. Depending on how bad it was, you might be sent to a different hatch and have it fumigated.'

⇦ ⇨ ⇦ ⇨ ⇦ ⇨

image opposite

Women that worked for Levers Bros.

'Then I worked the guano ships, bird droppings from them islands (off the coast of Peru). You had a five grain fork and you'd dig down and loosen her up with that and shovel it into bags. Everybody'd run for the ladder cause you had to get out from under it with the fumes. See, there was ammonia sprayed right through it as it was going aboard the ship, to save infection. The powder and the ammonia would burn your eyes and make you bleed from your nose. You used to put a handkerchief around your face to keep from breathing it. It was very hard to get men to go on them ships. Very, very hard. Men would only last one day. They'd get paid for that one day and they'd be gone.'

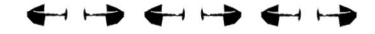

⇦ ⇨ ⇦ ⇨ ⇦ ⇨

'Outside work was a sort of easy job. It was harder for the men inside the lower holes. It was cruel hard work. It was no place for a clergyman's son, I can tell you that! Oh Christ, tough men, very tough. Toughest men in Ireland they were. We imported a lot of brown raw sugar and there was twenty-one stone in a bag and two men would lift that. Tough men. The hardest job in the lot was a pitch boat. This pitch stuff, it was real hot, like slacky coal, like tar, and they'd get all the by-products out of it. You used to have to go down and shovel it into tubs. The air off it would burn the eyes out of you and your nose burned. You used to have to wear a girl's stocking mask over your head. And the grain boats was hard because there was pollen off the grain, the dust. We used to bushel it into bags and that created a lot of dust powder. You inhaled it. It'd all gather in your chest. Dockers used to say, "take half a whiskey" and that seemed to ease it off. But you'd go home after four or five pints of porter and get a feed and the next morning you couldn't breathe. You'd get up and across there [points to chest] you'd think someone was after beating you with a hammer. The old grain porters, they died worse than the miners with lung trouble. They all died around their forties.'

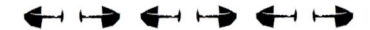

'A local lad was climbing up the ladder, it was near dinner hour. It was the last heave going out before they went for the dinner. And one piece of timber flew out and it scalped him. He died. They took him away in the ambulance.'

PADDY DALY

It was always a source of amazement to me that the amount of near misses by way of 20' and 40' steel girders, of timber, lumber, bags of various material, and general cargo, that would fall because inexperienced men, totally untrained, were slinging cargo incorrectly, on a hit and miss basis. Was it any wonder then, that cargo was falling from height into a confined space. I believe it was not just a wonder but a miracle that more people were not injured, even killed. I believe too that the ambulance was a much more frequent visitor to the deep-sea docks than the lads indicated. The amount of accidents and the level of litigation cases would attest to that. The high level of litigation cases put employers insurance premiums through the roof. At one stage, it was said that some men had several claims of various degree, some into the teens. This made it more difficult for the genuine man making a genuine claim.

The level of accidents did fall off considerably, but so too the volume of break-back cargo, and the facility to service that type of cargo. There was no more transit shed facility at North

DANGERS AND DEATHS

image

Two Coalmen by
Margaret Cullen
(Mairéad)

Wall extension, which was left dormant for many years, and slowly but surely the transit sheds at Ocean Pier were allowed to get beyond use. Leaking roof damage was allowed to go unchecked and unrepaired; together with massive pigeon and starling droppings, that put the sheds beyond use. So I suppose the lads were right to say the accident rate was not so high. Certainly at that time it wasn't. The lads told of men getting into an ambulance on the docks, and when it got to the traffic lights at Butt Bridge, they got out to head over to sign on in the labour exchange. They would get a lift back to the docks later. Meantime, when the ambulance arrived at the hospital, the doors were opened and there was nobody inside. You would, however, have a poor opinion of our ambulance service, to believe they would tolerate this happening on a regular basis. Dockers may joke about this and that, but they know, that the quick response of our ambulance service, their skill and expertise, had over the years, saved many a life, and I believe, that includes mine. Many years ago, working for a company called Conway Shipping, I suffered a serious head wound. The doctor in Jervis St. Hospital told me later, but for the knowledge of the paramedic at the scene, I would be dead. So a belated big thank you to that man, and on behalf of many of my ex-colleagues whom you served, and perhaps, like me, even saved. Thank you.

Well done you men and women, you do a great job. Paddy Daly.

image opposite

Heavy lifting in the hatch

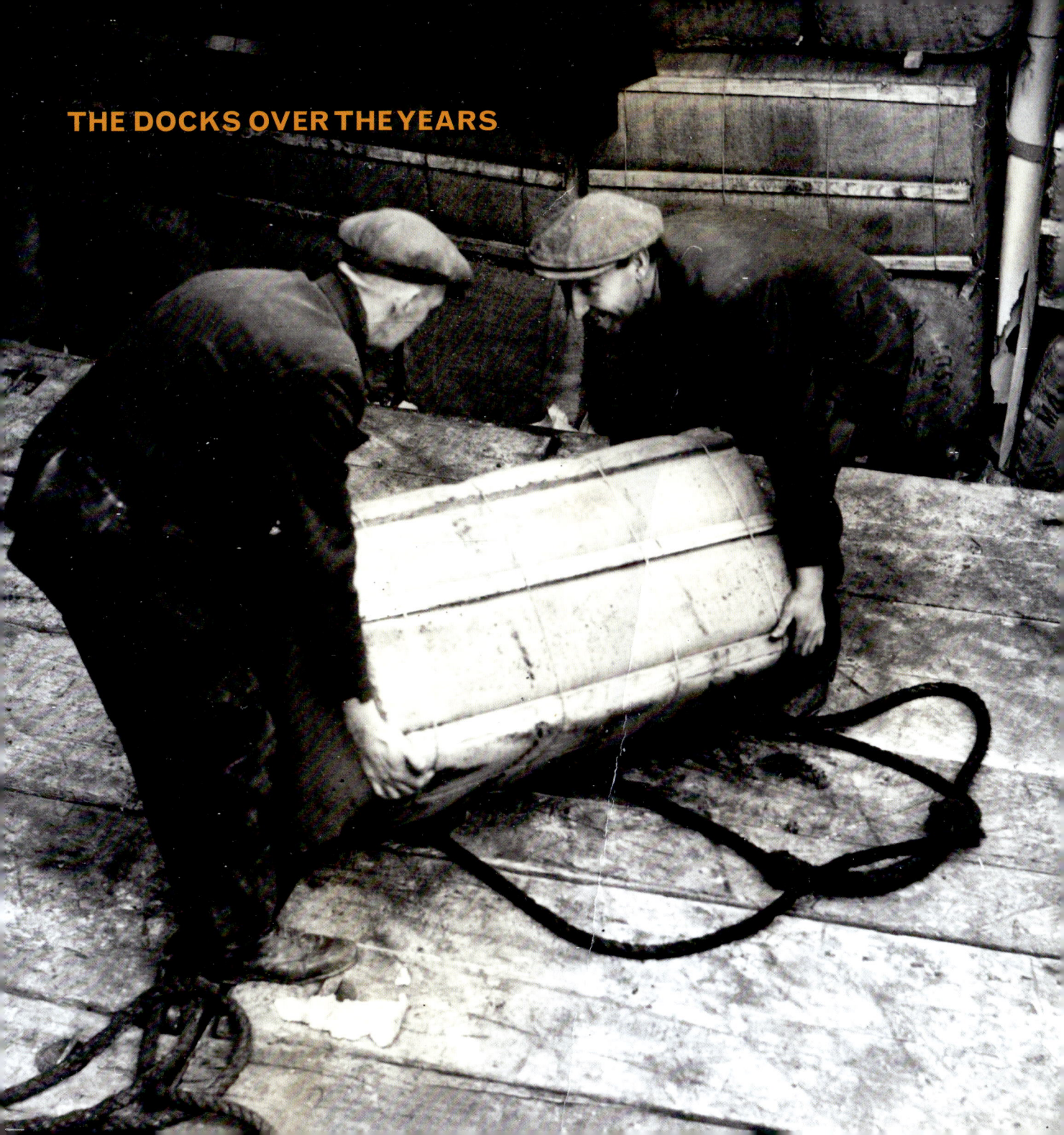

THE DOCKS OVER THE YEARS

DUBLIN PORT DIARIES

WILLIE MURPHY

'The docks in my young days... it was magic. My father was a docker and my grandfather was a shipwright and me great grandfather was a seagoing captain. I was born on Fitzwilliam Street (Ringsend) and I loved being around the docks. In them days there'd be horses going in all directions. And cobblestones, the square setts. That's what the whole docks was. And heavy trucks with steel frames and wooden handles pulled by men. Big, thick heavy steel wheels. Two men pushing and a man doing the "horse" as we called it. Everything was manual. Really hard, tough work.'

THE STORIES OF CHRISTOPHER DALY AND HIS GRANDFATHER, PATRICK 'COCKER' DALY,
as told by Christopher Daly

Christopher's father worked for the ESB (Electricity Supply Board), but his grandfather, Patrick 'Cocker' Daly, was a docker and legendary All Ireland winning Dublin footballer. Christopher brought along his grandfather's travel permit from 1941, which was photocopied to keep with Christopher's files. The travel permit incorrectly records his grandfather's date of birth as 1894, which would have made him only 6 years old when he won his first All Ireland Final! He was actually born in 1868. 'The Cocker' Daly won three All Ireland finals and seven Senior Championship Finals. He played club football with St Laurence O'Toole's, Parnell's, and the Geraldines. Brendan Behan, writing in the *Evening Herald*, stated that it was a great privilege to have seen 'The Cocker' Daly play.

Christopher's grandfather was a very strong man who worked a variety of jobs on the docks. Christopher especially remembered him working coal and cattle boats. 'The Cocker' Daly did not tolerate bullies and easily won respect. When he died in 1951, *The Irish Press* published his obituary on their front page, and he had one of the largest funerals ever seen in Dublin.

Christopher worked hard all his life. He started working on the docks in 1958 when he was 18 years of age. An East Wall native, he had spent the previous four years in England, having gone there at age 14 for work. He worked in England for a company that used massive ovens to smoke bacon. He remembered the terrific heat of the ovens. After working there for a few months, a person wouldn't have a pick of flesh on them. He remembered a man from Coventry with a big belly starting there. After five or six weeks he had lost all the weight from sweating in the extreme heat.

When Christopher decided to go to the docks for work it took three weeks for him to be first selected. He got up at 5:30 am to get the docker bus for 7:25 am to be at the docks for 7:55 am. He remembered his first bus journey and he recognised a lot of the men making the same journey from where he lived. Christopher's family lived on Strandford Road, East Wall, next to the Constantines, the Dalys, the Powers, and O'Mearas. People did not immediately recognise him for 'The Cocker' Daly's grandson but when he told them his name they quickly made the connection. Christopher was very proud of this. Christopher's first job was on a Sunday boat. The boat was empty and needed to be loaded. While Christopher had been on a boat many times before with his grandfather, he did not realise how deep the ship's hold was. When he looked down the open hatch, he got the fright of his life. Christopher wasn't too tired after his first day as he was used to hard physical labour.

Christopher went on to work for a variety of companies on the docks, including Murphy's, RA Burke, Newman's, and George Bell. Bell mostly employed the Ringsend dockers.

Christopher worked with fine chaps on the docks and enjoyed his working life. His best friends were Mike Byrne and Harry Coleman. Christopher didn't get any training for his job and had to work out for himself the best way to load or unload. You could make it difficult or make it handy. With bag work, the best thing to do is to sink down into the load until some of it is over you, so that you can unload it that way, then keep rearranging the load so that you are pulling the bags off a tier. You climb down into the load until it's up to your shoulder, clear what's above you, then dig down again. 'Dappy' Hayes showed him how to move a timber load to avoid accidentally smashing his hand.

All the men Christopher knew who worked in coal are dead. Christopher said that the coal dust was very dangerous.

Christopher wore jeans to work. One day he had a job unloading phosphate powder in South Wall. He got the ferry across the Liffey for a penny. The phosphate powder was loose, like sand in the Sahara. Men were coughing as they worked and soon enough were coughing blood. Average pay was 30 shillings a day. For this job you got an extra 5 shillings 'dirty money.' That job took 3 days. Men worked stripped to the waist. When he returned home,

Christopher's mother wanted to wash his jeans. Christopher told her to leave the jeans hanging outside for the moment. Three days later, the jeans were completely rotten.

Christopher's father-in-law worked on that ship too. He was 66 when he died, which was considered a good innings.

Too much talking and distractions were discouraged by the foremen as the crane hook was never to be left hanging waiting for a heave. Younger men were mindful to help out the older men to keep up with the crane.

After so many years, pallets were introduced with the cargo. Palgrave Murphy's were the first to use forklifts. Eventually containerisation was introduced. All of these changes dramatically reduced the number of people working on the docks.

The hard work on the docks meant that Christopher was strong and fit enough to run the Dublin marathon in 1982 and 1983. However, as Christopher worked before pallets were used, his spine fused and his back got progressively worse. His surgeon in the Mater Hospital advised that he might end up in a wheelchair. However, Christopher stayed active to avoid this. He retired from the docks aged 46.

Christopher was sorry that there weren't any women dockers.

FROM THE SESSIONS

'When I went on the docks we were after having a big strike in 1925. The union imported labour from all over Ireland – scabs to take our jobs. When the scabs came in there was a killing.[11] Terrible! Real violence during the time. Police charged with their batons and hit the pickets. Knocked them to the ground and kicked them. Scabs was afraid to come out after finishing a coal boat so they used to sleep in the stables overnight and come out in the early morning to avoid confrontation with the pickets. See, in 1927 when I was starting, these men who scabbed it, they were on a list and had priority over us. Ah yes. They got this privilege cause they scabbed it. Of course, this created anger. You'd say, 'look at the scabby bastards going in.' Even when the strike was over, the stigma was still there. You'd get it brought up in a pub, especially when they'd get a few drinks in them. Calling them a scabby and the man would have to get out of the pub. You wouldn't drink with him. There were digging matches

[11] *One man killed another with a hurling stick out of anger*

all over the place. Even in the hulls of ships. They'd come to punching one another. In them days it was just fists. There was no iron bars or knives or anything used. It be bare hands. Just make a ring and let them have it. No one would interfere. Let the best man win, it'd be settled. But the stigma never died. And it's still going on. People have memories and they still bring it up to their sons.'

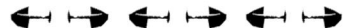

'The Second World War was a fiasco. Hitler's submarines was all around. Ah Christ, there was nothing here at all in the war years. The grass grew on the docks. The only thing we used to do was a bit of turf on our own boats from the bogs. Turf boats used to come in but with no coal. Nothing was coming in. So a lot of dockers joined the British army and we near all went to England to work. I went over and started building airfields around the midlands. After the war in 1945, I came home right back to the docks 'cause it was improving all the time. There was work. I was on the Red Cross and cattle boats, trying to save Europe. They fitted out them Liberty ships for cattle. There'd be Red Cross stuff down in the lower hole and between decks would be all cattle pens. A boat would hold 750 head of cattle. I seen more cattle in one day than a farmer would see in his lifetime. Plenty of horses were being sent away to the continent. Drovers would bring the cattle and horses down. Drovers and dockers got on very well. We were married to one another's sisters and brothers and we were all intermixed. Drovers and dockers, they'd drink together and everything. But drovers was lower than dockers … and that was low enough! I worked on the cattle boats as what you called a bullock man, to look after the cattle and milk the cows. It was a three day trip to Amsterdam and the cattle had to be milked, watered, and fed. There was one man that had to look after thirty cattle.'

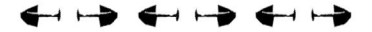

'I saw the end coming a long time before it came. And I even told others. It started first about 1961 with palletising the cargo, putting it on pallets and just lifting it up, a ton or two on a pallet. And then the forklift trucks for just going under the pallet and running it into the shed. Then small thirty foot containers coming in. Then they wanted gangs reduced – "too many men on the docks." They started realising what has happened here then. The crisis came around 1971 when we lost at least 250 men in one go. And now it's gone. It's terrible. Sad. The atmosphere is not there anymore… the old craic we used to have when we'd put out in a day. It was a part of history and now it's not there. I go over there and now, to me, it's a graveyard.'

JOHN 'MILEY' WALSH

In the early nineties, Dublin Charge Handling decided their marriage with the deep-sea dockers was over. They liquidated the company in a way that surely had to be against the law. As the parent company they had astronomical assets, but they were directed by one of the most corrupt governments this country has ever seen. We were on the labour once again, only this time not for a day or two, but if they had their way, for eternity. Liquidation is an impossible opponent to do battle against; it's tediously slow to get anything done, and the frustrations of waiting for decisions to be made in offices of the appointed bodies are torturous.

However, we are resourceful people and stubborn as mules and during the period we were out, April to December of 1992, several offers were made to groups and individuals to return to work under shady circumstances, but not one docker applied for those positions. They stood together to a man. We were forced to enlist in FÁS[12] before any kind of payment would be paid because we were in limbo as far as the authorities were concerned. We were not on strike, because we had no employer to picket. We were not entitled to job seekers allowance, because we maintained we were the only workers entitled to operate on the docks when and if it reopened.

By December, several legitimate companies appeared to have got the old stevedoring license back. A system was put in place whereby companies would take on dockers on a permanent basis according to the work they had. Others would form a group to hire and fire on their requirements for each day. It was certainly not ideal but it was considered better than nothing.

My offer of employment came from an old comrade Jerome Donleavy who I had worked with in Dublin Maritime. He represented a businessman named Ted O'Neill, who advanced us 500 quid in anticipation of a fair and decent working relationship and so it turned out. We got on very well with the crew he had picked, and once again I began to enjoy getting out of bed to go to work. The next years were both enjoyable and fruitful for both parties, until Mr. O'Neill sold the company to the Mersey Docks and Harbour Board. They arrived with a reputation for being a no-nonsense employer, but after a short time we found them to be if not as generous in the first days as Mr. O'Neill. They were reasonable employers.

For several years we worked under the guidance of Mersey docks until something appeared on the stock market in London, without so much as a hint we were taken over by Peel Ports.

[12] *An Foras Áiseanna Saothair – the Training and Employment Authority*

This company, I have to say, provided me with my worst experiences of working anywhere ever. They looked for confrontation at every juncture. Nothing we did here in Ireland was done the right way, despite our discharge rate and loading speed being superior to theirs in nearly all of their other operations, and their other holdings were substantial.

There was an inevitability about the break-up of relations when everything constantly required the Labour Court to sort out tiny, little problems that had previously only needed a five minute chat. Day after day, the workforce were put under more and more pressure with silly demands and cuts to wages. They only knew one way and that was to go for the jugular.

When the confrontation came and led to a major strike, every phase of the arbitration within the Labour Relations Council was won by the workers, but never accepted by the company. I find the next episode very hard to mention as it contains for me a sickening memory of some colleagues passing by our picket and working with scabs recruited from the company's other terminals in Belfast, Liverpool, and Glasgow.

The measure of the company's belligerent attitude was evident in their appointment of a security firm named Control Risks, a firm of mercenaries, ex-S.A.S.[13] soldiers and others. They turned up in the Labour Court with the manager one day to negotiate with us. Of course we refused to negotiate with them, as we believed them to be carrying guns or other weapons. The head man at the labour court was Kieran Mulvey who was highly annoyed with us and refused to believe us about them being armed, but was gobsmacked when we pointed to them in the carpark searching under their cars for bombs.

That period of unrest was my worst ever experience on the docks. At the beginning, when the work was sometimes intolerably hard, there was a sense of achievement or a satisfaction in having pushed your body to its limits – but there is no job satisfaction in being treated like a foreigner in your own country.

[13] *Special Air Service of the British Army*

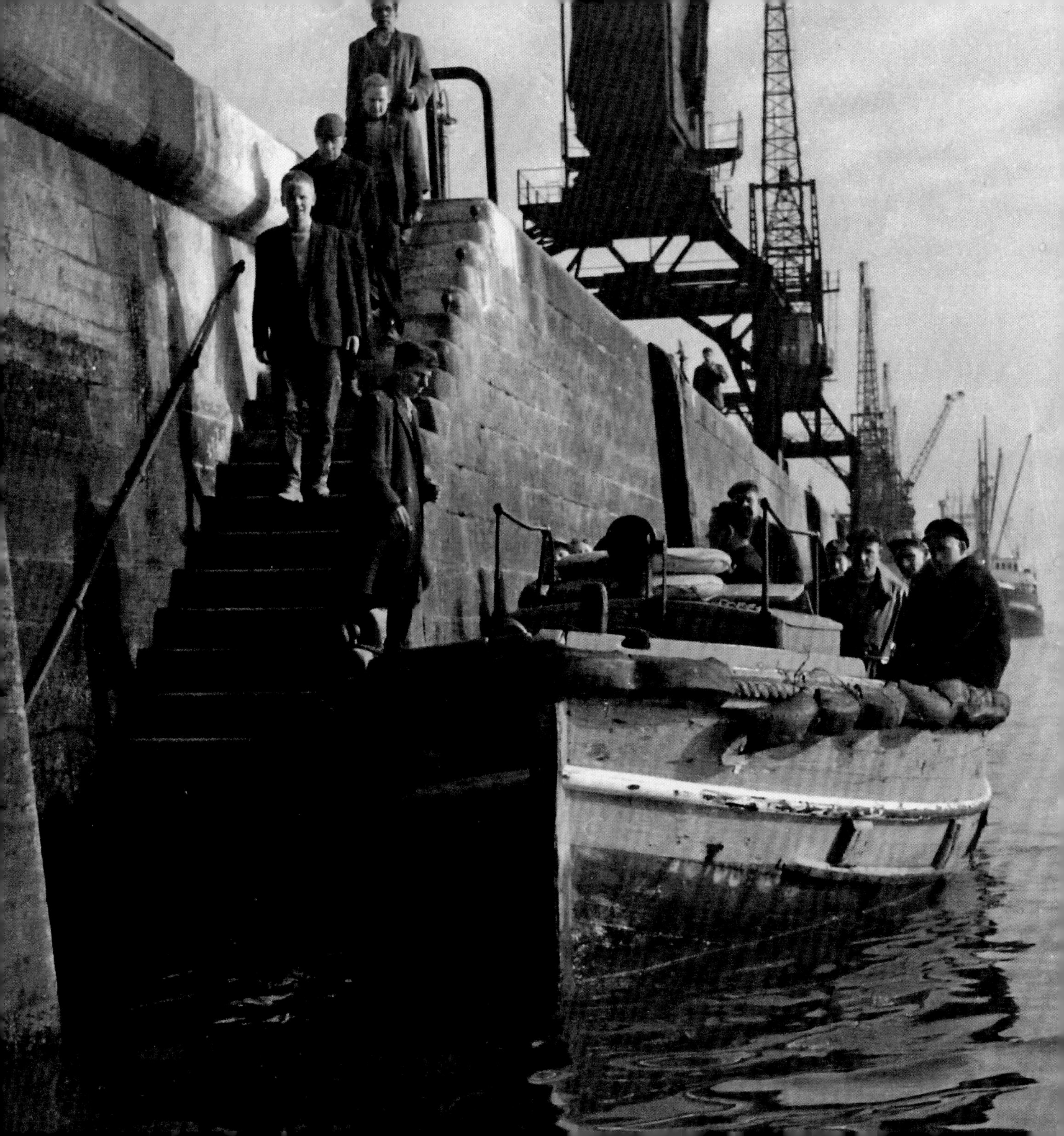

'LIFE ON THE DOCKS'
by Richard Saunders

I am not a docker, but I spent most of my life working on and rowing in Dublin Port. At ten years of age, I joined the Dodder Sea Scouts where I learned seamanship, rowing and knots. I left the scouts at fourteen years old and joined St. Patrick's Rowing Club, where I remain today and I am currently the club chairman.

As a young boy of fourteen years, I helped the lock keepers with the opening and closing of the sea lock grand canal basin for ships arriving and departing. It was hard work, so the lock keepers were glad of the help and it was my way of being near ships. At that early age it was now in my mind to go to sea, on deck if possible. Mr Mullen who was the lock keeper at the time had connections with the Seaman Union of Ireland.

He gave my name, and at the age of sixteen I was appointed Deck Trainee on the Irish Alder which was situated in Bremen, Germany trading on the North Atlantic run. I was promoted to ordinary seaman after just seven months. I never came into Dublin on this ship, but I came in contact with the Dublin dockers when I joined the cattle boat Diana Clausen trading Dublin to Hamburg. And then when I arrived into Dublin from Brazil on the Irish spruce with cattle feed, on the Irish Poplar on the Dublin to New York run, the Irish Cedar trading Dublin to Casablanca, and finally the MV[14] Cameo, a coaster trading into the Eurozone.

I kept up my contact with the lock keepers and when home on leave in the summertime. I relieved all the crew for their annual leave and I think it was three times that brought me working for CIÉ (Córas Iompair Éireann) as they were in charge of all the canals.

When home on leave from the Irish Cedar in 1968, I was asked by Kevin Curry, Marine Superintendent for Dublin Corporation owners of the Liffey Ferries (or Docker Ferries as they were known), to drive the Ferries. At that time I think the Ferry Number 6 was sunk by the British Rail Cattleship – The Slieve League and the ferry driver had went sick. Thankfully no one was injured in that sinking.

I started the job the next day and worked for ten months on the ferries, and also on the MV Shamrock for repairs in Pigeon House Harbour. At this time I still had a longing to go back to sea and seeing the Irish shipping vessels coming in and out of Dublin Port started to get me on edge.

It was at that point that I had to make a big decision. I made a choice to leave Dublin

image
The Liffey Boat AKA The Docker's Taxi

14
Motor Vessel, used as a prefix for ship names

Corporation and joined the New Irish Elm a bulk carrier and car carrier, which carried up to 2,500 cars on world-wide trading.

I started working for Dublin Port in 1977 where my first job was lock keeper at Custom's House Dock North Wall. Then I was the Graving Dock Gateman at Alexandra Quay then the berthing master, then I was coxswain on the police boat and able seaman on the tugs. However, it was as the Pilot Boat Coxswain where I spent 25 years. The last ten years we spent training all of the marine staff in the new pilot boats twin screws – speed 25 knots. For me this was like going back to school to train for Dublin V.T.S. radio (Vessel Traffic Service).

I then started training for the Officer of the Watch certification for the tugs and their engine operations. The last three years were spent working on the new tugs with only a two man crew and the engine horsepower was 5,500 which was nearly the same horsepower as the engines on the Irish Alder where I earlier worked as a deck trainee in 1963.

In 2008 the hull of the Liffey Ferry came into my ownership. She was lying in the graving dock Alex basin and was about to be scrapped. I had a word with my son Barry who is a welder/fabricator, and we both agreed to take on the job. He was sorry in the end as it took nearly fours years to complete. Charlie Murphy of Dublin Port Company got me permission to work on the ferry for as long as it took, with electricity supplied.

In 2010, the No. 9 Liffey Ferry was going for scrap and had been lying in the Ringsend dockyard since 1985. Not one bit of work done to preserve her! I took the cab off the No. 9 ferry and repaired it in St. Patrick's Rowing Club. So what we have now is the hull of No. 11 ferry and the cab off No. 9 ferry.

Upon completion, we obtained a license for twelve passengers to run on the River Dodder, Grand Canal and the Royal Canal. No licence was obtained for the Liffey as the hull is open plan, no air tanks. My aim in the first place was to save the ferry from scrapping and to save it for the maritime history of Dublin Port.

The working crew was as follows:

Richard Saunders

Barry Saunders (Son)

Stephen Saunders (Son)

Ajmal Saunders (Grandson)

Suggested name for the ferry coming from my wife: DIVORCE!

FATHERS

'THE GREAT PROVIDER'
by Mick Foran

Oh how I long to be with that man, digging for cockles on Sandymount Strand,
He brought me everywhere on the cross-bar of his bike,

And explained everything in detail about the values of life.
He was warm and gentle and also kind, and could always tell what was on your mind!

He brought home food & coal from the Docks, by hook or by crook it had to be got!

The Great Provider

JIMMY MCLOUGHLIN

Jimmy McLoughlin never worked on the docks, but his Dad did and he heard many stories from his mother and others in subsequent years.

Jimmy went away to England when he was fifteen on the Princess Maud boat around 1954/55 and returned to Dublin in 1974. He got a job in Pearse Street Library, and while going through old newspapers he came across an image of his Dad and a colleague taken on Dollymount Strand when they were dockers.

Jimmy became interested in the world of the dockers. His Dad had been a fisherman from Howth who met a woman one night in Dublin city, and married her a week later. Because he married outside his community he became known as 'The Dublin Kid.' If the weather was bad his Dad would go to the reads around six o'clock in the morning, and more often than not come back saying 'nothing today' and 'the fucking button men.'

He recalls it being a hard life, his family never had much. There was eight of them living in one room with an outside toilet, and he spoke of the sadness of his mother. He said his Dad would get paid in the pub and by the time he came home there wouldn't be much money left. Jimmy himself was an alcoholic and through attending Alcoholics Anonymous meetings he met many former dockers and heard their stories.

RICHARD 'BOXER' ELLIOT

'Well, me father was a boxer. See, the dockers opened a boxing club. They opened their own boxing club. He was a founding member. The docks were my playground since I was a kid. From the day I was born, me dream was to work on the dock. All different cargo, everything. Even though I didn't have a button at the time, my Dad gave me his. That was later. The one button wouldn't serve the two.'

FROM THE SESSIONS

'Paddy Fitzpatrick, the son of a Dublin docker, became a priest — and the only docker's son that anyone ever heard about becoming a priest. The day he was ordained, his father went in the toilets. One of the priests there said to him, "I believe the new priest's father is a doctor." His father said, "ah yes," and walked right out.'

'Dockers liked betting, and every day I had to bring the midday racing paper. He wouldn't eat his dinner if he hadn't got that. Every day my Da had what they called a rapple, a few bob — like you were betting tuppence and sixpence. Oh, I used to be a runner for me father. Bookies were illegal but they'd come down the dock steps out of sight of the police and take the bets. All the dockers would bet with them. So he'd look through the racing paper and pick out the horse and write it out and I'd bring it across to the bookie. And maybe the next day he'd say, "there's so much coming back." We had an altar in the corner of the room at home, a small altar liked the Blessed Sacred Heart, and a red light burning and an altar cloth underneath. Well, he'd say, "put it under the altar cloth" and he'd know where it'd be when he'd come home.'

'My first memories was carrying my father's dinner over there. I was eight years old. All the sons did that. That was the ritual in them days. It was a 1:00 pm bell and you had to be there, dead on. There was a rowboat bringing the dockers from Ringsend over to the North Wall, so I was rowed across with his dinner for a penny each way. It might have been a coddle put in a bowl and there'd be a saucer to fit over the top so it was enclosed. And wraped up with a

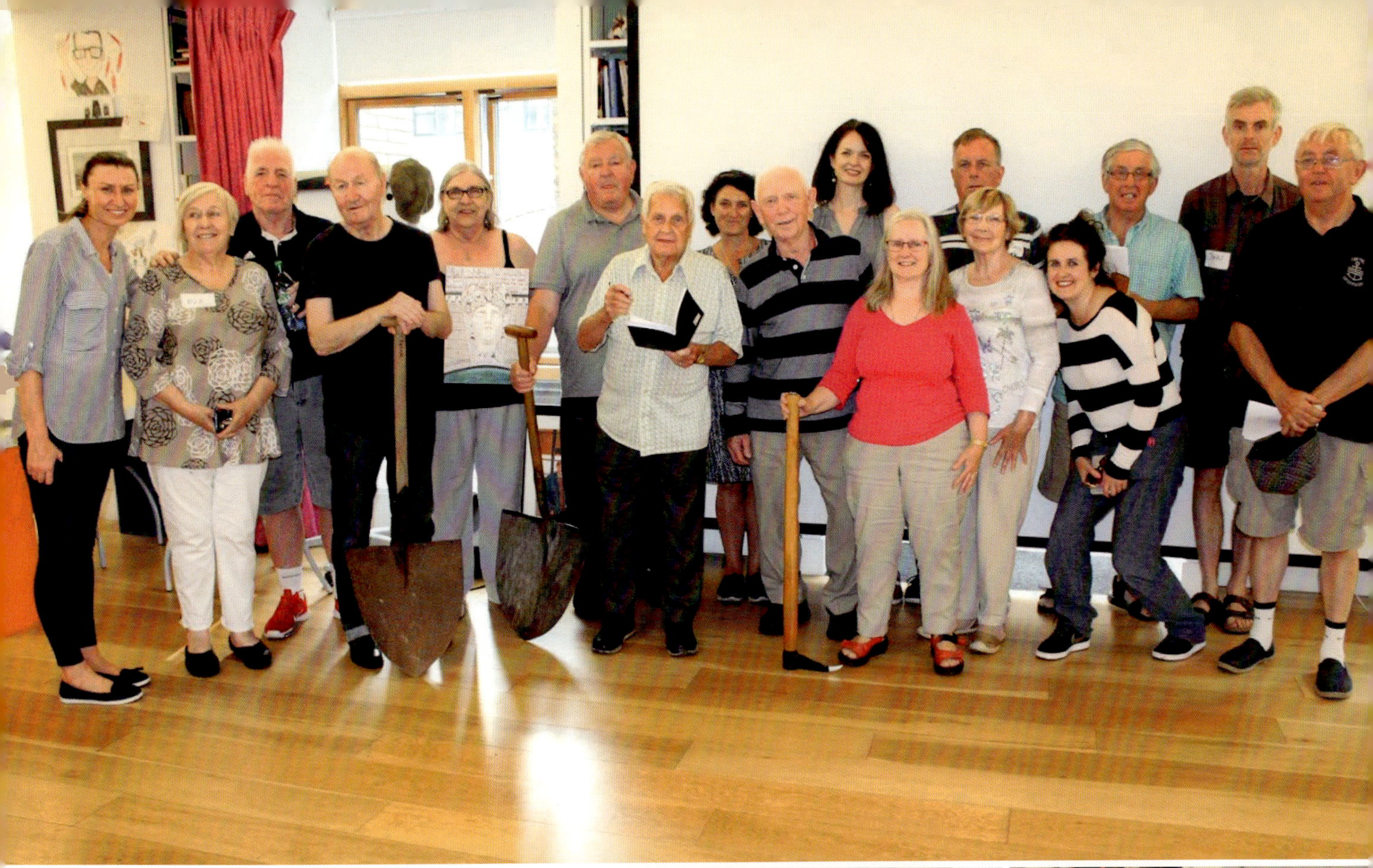

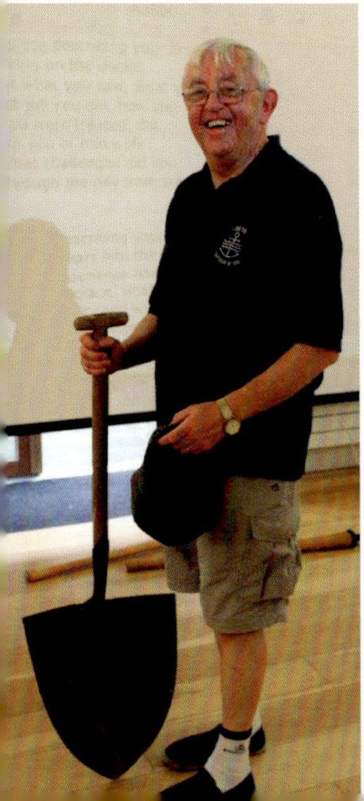

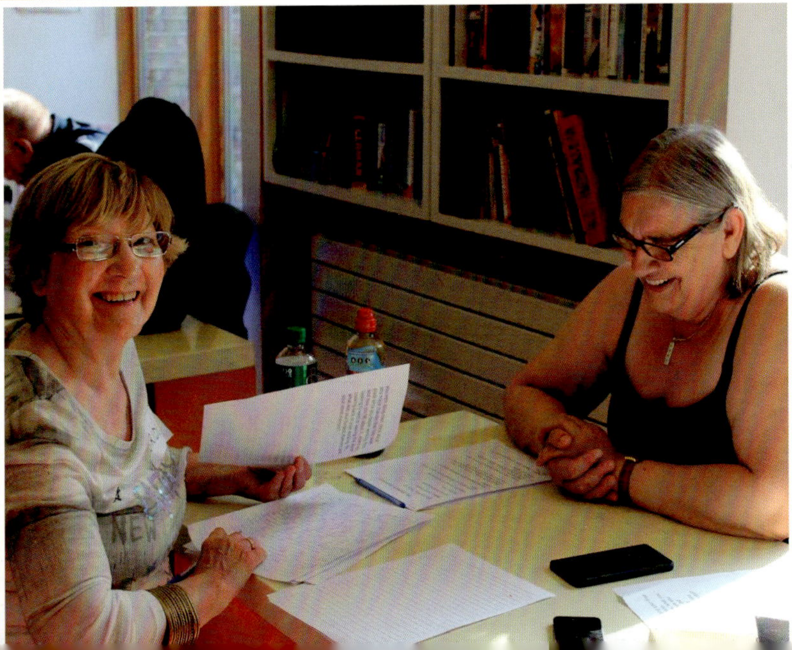

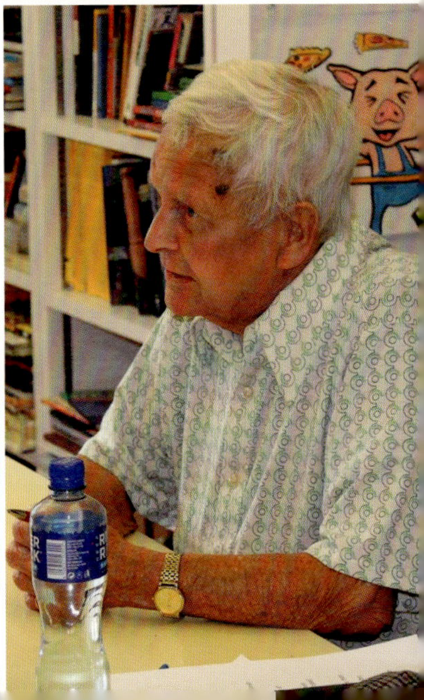

Retired dock workers with their families and volunteers at a workshop at Fighting Words

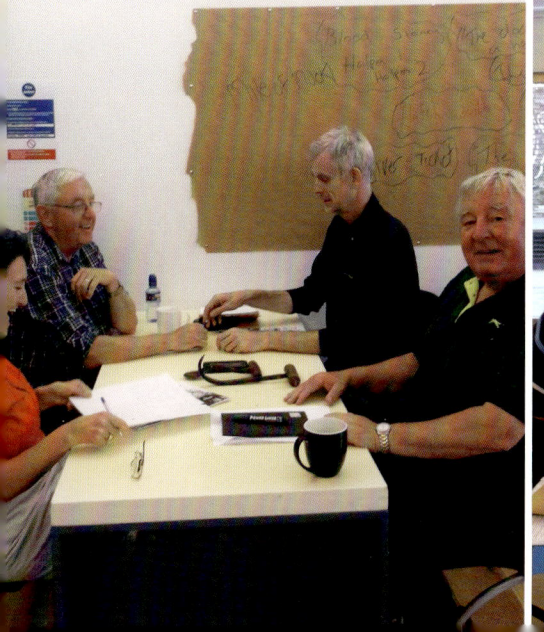

woman's woollen sock around it that kept it warm. And then a red handkerchief with white spots. In those days the men tied them around their neck to keep the sweat from coming down, then use it for wiping the sweat off the brow. That was always washed and cleaned, a priority that it was a fresh handkerchief going over his dinner. He'd be waiting on the deck of the ship. An old galvanised tea can holds about a pint — with a grain ship maybe I'd get to fill a can and bowl full of grain and corn coming back. All the people around this area had hens and they'd give me tuppence for a bowl of grain and tuppence for a can of corn. So that's the way we'd get our ferry money and we'd make a few coppers from that.'

PADDY MOONEY: PAINTER & DOCKER
by Marie Fallon

Born on Glouster Street, behind City Quay Church, Paddy Mooney started his working career in the Gaiety, Gate, and Abbey theatres, as had his brother before him. Working with the scenic artist, his drawing and painting skills were recognised. Paddy attended the National College of Art and Design, then located on Kildare Street, as a night student studying under Sean Keating amongst others.

He was then working as a scenic artist. He was to work with Michael O'Herlihy and Dan O'Neill. Paddy married in 1954 but within a few years, with a mortgage and a family of three, Paddy sought an increase in salary. This was not forthcoming. Paddy's father had been a docker and tradition at the time ensured that the button worn by the father could be passed to the son. Paddy took the button and started work on the docks.

For the next 20 years he worked on the docks.

A meeting with Seamus Redmond started a new phase in his life. Seamus was heavily involved with the Marine Port and General Workers' Union. He was also an artist and lover of painting. Seamus held exhibitions with work from members of the union in various locations. Paddy became involved, and his work sold out at the shows. Exhibitions were held in the Marine Port Union offices and the Port and Docks Board.

Paddy sadly died in 1984 but his legacy lives on in his family. His daughter Marie Fallon is a professional artist and works with North Dublin Mental Health services as an arts facilitator His grandson Paul graduated from the National College of Art and Design in 1996.

'SKIPPER' DUNNE

Skipper was given his nickname around the age of twelve. Being that he was older than the other local kids, visiting sailors would ask him to come up and guard the gang plank. The kids gave him the name of Skipper. All of his children (sons and daughters) were subsequently known as Skipper.

Skipper went on to become a docker, and his son recollects him having the bunkering[13] on the inside of his coat. He would come home and empty out his inside big pockets onto a newspaper on the floor. Loose tea leaves would empty out onto the paper, along with splinters from the wooden chest that had been smashed open with a hook.

His son also worked in a bar by the docks, and he remembers receiving a phone call saying that there was a boat docked and dockers were working late. They would have a one hour break and they would be coming over for some refreshments. He was told to 'just start pulling pints of Guinness, and keep pulling them!' When the dockers came in they drank eight pints each within an hour. They put their money on the table and left to go back. Skipper's son said, 'It was thirsty work, working on the docks.'

[15] *Large pockets sewn into the inside of dockers' coats; used for smuggling cargo*

MARGARET CULLEN

'My father was a button man. He was gone to work before you got up. Gone all day. Being a button man, he worked most days. There was nine in our family, three boys and six girls. Some days he didn't come home early due to overtime on the boats.

He was a singer-out: William Byrne for the company Palgrave Murphy. He was known as 'Glimmer' but there was no known reason for his nickname. Once, he brought home green bananas, He put them inside clothing in a press to ripen but me and my brother and sister ate them when they were still green.

My father loved history. He would talk to me about lots of different stuff. We shared that in common – I love history too. He talked a lot about the 1916 Rising. One story he often told was that the Black and Tans got a call about a disturbance in a pub. When the Black and Tans arrived in an open truck, they parked under the Railway Bridge opposite the pub. A bomb was thrown from the bridge onto the truck.'

Margaret has no memory of the rest of the story, whether people were killed or maimed. Margaret's father criticised DeValera and was unhappy that Dev didn't suffer the consequences of the Rising when all around him were shot or imprisoned. She did remember that her father got her youngest brother a job in Colfix, producing either oil or tar.

'THE OLD MEN AND THE SEA'
by Mick Foran

Back in the 1950s I was brushing up on my Catechism, as I was getting ready to receive my First Holy Communion in a couple of weeks time. My father let a shout into the bedroom 'You better hurry up, or the tide will catch us out!'

'Alright Da, I'm finished!' I replied, walking out of the bedroom.

My father was pumping up the wheels of his old bike, getting ready to bring me with him. Every summer we went to Sandymount to dig for cockles, especially when he wasn't working on the docks, as he only got casual work. Times were tough in Dublin, and Sheriff Street was a poor place to live.

But we were very lucky. My father could turn his hand to anything – he could fix old radios, fix old bikes; he could also paint and decorate. And when he was working the docks, maybe digging coal boats, he would always bring home a bunker of coal in his saddle bag, or maybe some loose tea or tinned fruit or tinned salmon. We never experienced a hungry day. If I asked my father about the swag he would say, 'It fell of the back of a lorry, son,' or sometimes he would mumble to himself, 'to the victor the spoils.' That's the type of man he was.

So off we went, but this time in the saddle bag we had one onion sack and two old spoons for digging cockles. We finally arrived at the Martello Tower at Sandymount and I was glad to jump off the crossbar and rub my backside. The sun was splitting the sky and the tide was miles out at sea. My Da said, 'right, son – let's make hay while the sun shines.' We left the bike against the wall and took off our shoes and socks and started that long walk out to the water's edge. We spotted some of the old men we knew from previous digs. They greeted us with a big wave of their hands. Eventually everyone was on their knees digging for cockles, and one of the old men showed me the best way to find the cockles under the sand. He said, 'dig between the ripples of the sand – now, you try it,' and I did and it worked perfect. Then the conversation began about

1916-1921 and the IRA and the Black and Tans and who ambushed the Tans in Dublin. This went on for a good while, and I just sat there on my hunkers listening to everything.

Time passed and we had about two stone of cockles in the sack and the tide was starting to come in around us. My father said, 'I think it's time to retreat, Jim. The tide has beaten us.'

Old man Jim said, 'but sure, tomorrow is another day. Anyway, I think we have plenty.' We all walked back together to the Martello Tower. A small trapped lake of sea water lay about one hundred feet away from the tower. The men put the sacks of shellfish into the water and dragged the sacks up and down the lake in order to wash the excess sand from the bag. That's why they used onion sacks.

It was evening time. We all said goodbye to each other. My father said to me, 'right, son – we better saddle up and ride into the sunset. I think Mrs. Foran will be worried about us.' Sometimes my father would refer to my mother as Mrs. Foran, but mostly Mary-Ann. We made our way along the coast road. The sun was going down fast. We went to the customs house and onto the cobblestones. I managed to look back at the saddle bag. The sea water was dripping onto the stones. I thought we'd never get home. I said to my father, 'hey Da, did that old man Jim really ambush the Black and Tans?'

'Oh, yes. I know that man a long time – he knew your grandfather well, but they took different sides during the Civil War. Thank God they never met each other at the time. By God your ears were well cocked, ye don't miss a thing.'

We finally got back to the flats where we lived. My father put the cockles into the throw and washed the remaining sand out of them and my mother put them on to boil. I went into the bedroom to read an old comic I had. About one hour later, my father brought me in a small plate of steaming hot cockles and two slices of brown bread and a mug of tea. They tasted lovely.

Many years later, I often stopped at the Martello Tower and looked out to sea, hoping to glimpse the old men waving to me. I'll never forget those beautiful days I spent with my father, that lovely quality time we spent together, and never forgetting.

DUBLIN PORT DIARIES

PRIMARY SCHOOL STORIES

John 'Miley' Walsh, Paddy Nevins and Declan Byrne visited two Fighting Words primary school workshops and gave the students a brief history of life on the docks, and shared some of their own experiences. They then asked the children to create a story that took place on the docks. Following the Fighting Words format, the students created the first half of the story together, and then wrote their own endings. The following pieces are the collaborative first halves of their stories.

STEVE 'NO SHOES' AND TIC-TAC

St Laurence O'Toole's Boys National School, 4th & 5th Class, 8 March 2019

It was a cold snowy night in work at the docks for Steve 'No Shoes.' The water was icy. His toes were freezing. And there was an icicle stuck to the end of his nose.

Steve 'No Shoes' went home after work. Before he went to bed, he wished to get a new pair of shoes.

The next day, Steve's best friend Tic-Tac knocked on his door. Tic-Tac asked, 'Do you have any spare change so that I can buy some Tic-Tacs?'

'No. I can't even afford a pair of shoes,' replied Steve.

'Okay, I'll see you at work later,' said Tic-Tac.

A newspaper came through the door. There was an advert for the latest shoes at half price! Steve 'No Shoes' went into work and he nearly fell into the water. That was his worst fear.

Steve 'No Shoes' asked his boss for extra hours so that he could afford the shoes…

illustration by Zoe Canin

DUBLIN PORT DIARIES

THE CANAL MAN

Ringsend Boys National School, 3rd & 4th Class, 10th May 2019

Long, long ago, there lived a man called Billy who was always falling into the canal. One day when he had fallen into the canal, he found a teapot.

There was a little baby water-snake in the teapot. Then he heard the thumping of his boss coming towards him.

'Oh shoot, the boss is coming! I better look like I didn't fall into the canal,' said Billy to himself.

When the boss came, he saw the teapot. 'What's in there?' he asked.

'Nuttin'!' said Billy. 'I was just collecting water.'

The boss asked, 'What is the water for?'

'I was gonna drink it,' replied Billy.

There was another person in front of Billy.

'What's in that teapot?' demanded the mysterious man.

'Just water,' said the boss.

He roughly yanked the teapot out of Billy's hand and opened it to find the water-snake.

The water-snake bit the boss on the nose.

With that, Billy yanked back the teapot and ran off with the water-snake.
The boss chased Billy.

Billy saw a boat and ran into it to hide. The boss couldn't find him.

While he was in the boat, he named the snake Luigi. Later on, the boss called Billy to a meeting. His fat face was still red like a tomato and he clenched his fists and he tried to punch the snake.

Luigi was actually an alien from a different planet!

Time stopped for Billy and he thought of what could have happened if he had not fallen into the canal for once...

image

illustration by Areti Vasmatzoglou

PRIMARY SCHOOL STORIES

LAGGER REDMOND

THE LITTLE FLOWER

BRONCO DENNIS

FATSER DUNNE

NICKNAMES

Dublin dockers had many strange, fascinating nicknames. Reasons behind their nicknames ranged from hobbies to physical characteristics to memorable stories. Some nicknames passed around families from one docker to another. Richard 'Boxer' Elliot inherited his nickname from his father, who was a founding member of the dockers' boxing club. All of 'Skipper' Dunne's children were also named 'Skipper'– both sons and daughters. Nicknames were also inspired by relatives. One well-endowed docker was nicknamed 'Nudger;' consequently, his younger brother was unfortunately named 'Little Nudger.'

Most unrelated dockers didn't share nicknames, save for the handful of men nicknamed 'OXO.' These men were dubbed 'OXO' due to their inability to sign their own names on documents.

Most dockers' nicknames lasted for their entire career on the docks. Only rarely would a name be changed, as was the case of 'Daddy' Cahill. 'Daddy' Cahill became 'Mammy' Cahill after confessing to his mates that his wife threw his dinner over his head the night before for staying out late at the pub.

According to Paddy Daly, dockers could work with a man for years and yet never know what his Christian name was. Even the stevedores would call out dockers by nicknames at the read. At one read in particular, the stevedore called out for the docker 'Mousey.' 'Mousey' pushed his two sons forward so they could get the job. The stevedore replied, 'Not the mice – I'm looking for Mousey.'

The following list contains some of the many nicknames of the Dublin dockers.
The list was originally compiled by Paddy Daly, and added to over the course of various Fighting Words workshops.

image

Attending a workshop at the National Print Museum

B
Pop Barry/ Slasher Barry/ Bedah Behan/ Rommel Behan/ Bendego/ Swinger Bissett/ Trigger Bissett/ Mousey Boylan/ Earrings Bradley/ Jagger Brady/ Nipper Breslin/ Datsy Brown/ Slim Brown/ These'll Brown/ Jigger Buckley/ Mixer Breen/ Boo Byrne/ Blue Nose Byrne/ Clinkey Byrne/ Daddy Byrne/ Glimmer Byrne/ Man from Larame Byrne/ Nanier Byrne/ Ninety Byrne/ Oxo Byrne/ Saintey Byrne/ Shoulders Byrne/ St. Francis Byrne/ Yank Byrne

ATE THE BABBIE

WANDERLY WAGON

WAREWOLF FREEMAN

LAGGER REDMOND

SNARKEYE

THE LITTLE FLOWER

THE HAWK

FATSER DUNNE

THE HAWK

BRONCO DENNIS

C

Daddy Cahill AKA Mammy Cahill/ Bo Callaghan/ Count The Skulls Callaghan/ Crab Carberry/ Fibbey Carberry/ Bombardier Carass/ Eat The Baby Carass/ Ropes Carass/ Bosun Carrick/ Chadier Caulfield/ Terrier Caulfield/ Chinawang/ Saddler Cloake/ Cho Boy Coghlan/ Georgeous George Coghlan/ Nuggey Bar Connolly/ Coxey Corbally/ Saw Cox/ Marmo Coyle/ Foot and a half Culey/ Hardloaf Cummins/ Curger Cunnigham/ Canary Cullen/ Chappy Curley/ Fatse Currie

D

Butch Dardis/ Lats Dempsey/ Bronco Dennis/ Dickey Dennis/ Demon Dent/ Mittener Dent/ Rambler Dent/ Figio Dillion/ Bogey Dixon/ Jock Donaghue/ Mika Donnelly/ Toner Downey/ Bale Doyle/ Bat Doyle/ Big Apple Doyle/ Greek Doyle/ Me-did Doyle/ Muddler Doyle/ Little Apple Doyle/ Soldier Driscoll/ Beefer Duffy/ Torry Duffy/ Crongie Dunne/ Fatser Dunne/ Skipper Dunne

E

Leftie Egan/ Rusler Egan-Kearns/ Boxer Elliot

F

Pa Fagan/ Granny Farrell/ Fuucker Finn/ Lemons Fitzsimmons/ Straney Fitzsimmons/ Rolo Fullman/ Silent Pencil Fulham/ Valley Fulham/ Warewolf Freeman

G

Rubber Legs Gaffney/ Da Gaines/ Buffer Gannon/ Batch Green/ Bagey Grey/ Jockser Gibbs/ Fingers Grimes

H

Gabby Hayes/ Hawkie Hawkins/ Atlas Hughes/ Sandy Man Hughes/ Masher Hutch/ Hen Pullen/ Hole in the Head

J

Nucker Jones

K
Bimbo Keating/ Nudger Keating/ Big Nose Kelly/ Chester Kelly/ Chick Kelly/ Melter Kelly/ Little Big Nose Kelly/ Skinner Kelly/ Knock Out Kelty/ Miner Kennedy/ Genna King/ Gitters Kinsella/ DuckEgg Kirwan/ Knockout/ Kit Farrell A.K.A. Killer Farrell

L
Briney Lawless/ Brother Lawless/ German Lawless/ Little Nudger/ Long Balls/ Lousey Shoulders/ Gipen-Na Lynch

M
Meet Your New Mammy/ Bando Macken/ Baldo McAuley/ Battler McCann/ Buller McDonald/ Lee Wee McDonald/ Spike McDonald/ Snipes McDonald/ Follow the Corpse Mitten/ Blake Montgomery/ Monty Montgomery/ Dig In The Goo Mooney/ Great Lover Mooney/ Scumer Mulhall/ Heney Mullen/ Uncle Mullen/ Mousey/ Boy Murphy/ Gidda Murphy/ Gimp Murphy/ Guard Murphy/ Lacks Murphy/ Long Balls Murphy/ Muckler Murphy/ Lordy Murphy/ Two Thumbs Murphy/ Consor Murray

N
Whacker Nugent/ Nudger

O
Slat Box O'Connor/ Yoy Yoy O'Driscoll/ Nutsy O'Toole

Q
Biners Quinn

R
Lagger Redmond/ Toothins Redmond/ Canadian Joe Reilly/ Gannet Reilly/ Tucker Reilly/ Sonser Reilly/ Wire Robinson/ Nigger Ryan/ Oxo Roe/ Rubber Legs

S
Doggie Smith/ Blue Boy Stanton/ Oxo Sweeney

T
Tiddler Tierney/ The Billy Can Bomber/ The Polish Ambassador/ The German/ The Hen Pullen/ The Wicked Chicken

W
Bleeder Walsh/ Bushler Walsh/ Miley Walsh/ Gitchey Welch/ Bull Weldon

DOCKERS' DICTIONARY

A Sea of Cargo: Pronounced 'say'

Aul Hen, The: Wife

Bag Hook: Hook with multiple prongs which was specifically designed for even distribution; Dockers also referred to their wife as 'the bag hook'

Beero: Lunch-break

Big Nudger: Nickname for a well endowed man

Blood Wagon: Ambulance

Bogey: Four wheeled trolley

Bowler: Dog

Boozer: Pub

Bullockin': Transporting livestock

Bunkering: Filling coat pockets; women used to sew in secret pockets in the jackets of the dockers

Bru, The: Bureau Labour, now the Social Welfare Office.

Cargo Hook/Bale Hook: Used in many industries throughout the world; Pulled heavy hessian or sacks of flour.

Coalies: Dockers who worked specifically with coal (a particularly laborious job)

WIDOW MAKER   BEERO   BLOOD WAGON

Come up on it: Increase heavy load to finish faster

Crane Man: Man using a crane

Dana: Boats with a broad varied of shipments; inspired by 70s Eurovision winner with the song 'All Kinds of Everything'

Decasualisation: Added structured shifts to the working day

Derrick: Name for the beam of a crane.

Diesel Fitter, A: Thief – 'These will fit her'

Disneyland: Any pub

Dockers' Taxi: An Ambulance (Same phrase was used to describe The Liffey Ferry)

Dunnage: Embarrassment Money, Dirty Money or Hardship Money

Fall Back Pay: Guaranteed payment for permanent employees if no ships came into port (after decausalisation); about one third of days pay

Get up the yard, the lane is full!: To rebuff someone

Give it a lash: Hurry up!

Gull: Docker from Ringsend

Hammer-Man: A man who would open crates for customs inspections (AKA producer)

Hand-Me-Downer: Someone who inherited the button

Hector Greys: Blue Flannel Line (ship)

Hoggers: Would drink leftover Guinness from used kegs

Hurry Up Yoke: Ambulance

The Jacks: The Toilet

Large Hand Truck: Used by experienced dockers to transport timber

The Mot: Wife or girlfriend

Moving Statues: A gang of dockers not known for their hard work.

Nine: Men using hand trucks/bogies; three men to each truck/bogie

On the scrounge: Looking to borrow, scab, or steal

Overtime Gangs: Gangs who would work on the same vessel after the work day is finished

PB–Pox Bottle: A derogatory term to call someone

Pixelated: Away with the fairies

Podger: Plank used to put under a wheel to rock a truck to collect whatever falls off

Possin': Soaking wet, drenched

Prick-Relations: Closely related by blood

Put a shortner on that: (Command) To get cargo safely out of the hatch by tightening and tying ropes, chains, straps, or wires so that the cargo won't fall loose

Quare Fella, The: The Strange Man

Reefed: Torn

She/Her: Boat

Short Gang: Consists of one man on deck (singer-out), six men to sling the cargo, and two men landing cargo onto the transport

Singer-out: On deck directs the crane man; Uses signals and gives instructions. 'Inside forward (for'ard), inside (aft) after, inside mid-ship'

Six: Men inside the hold; cargo for crane discharge

Spell off: To sub in for someone

Stand in for loose: (Also: **Over your head for a ball of lead**) To step away (from under a hoist); urgent – something is loose; Sometimes dockers would loosen a crate and allow it to fall and smash, so that they could retrieve the contents; The man operating the crane would shout, 'Stand in for loose' to let the others know what was happening and to protect themselves

Stevedore: Man in charge of assigning jobs to dockers

Stitcher: Repairs bags that 'get reefed'

Timber Gang: Singer out, six inside men, nine bogey men – three on each bogey, two tierers, two toppers

Top up the gib: Bring the top of the gib crane upwards and back towards the dock

Two: Men responsible for stacking timber or general cargo to a regulation height

Unsacked: Rehired

Widow Maker: Lead ball that posed a threat

Working Gangs: A set of people who would work on a singular vessel until unloading/loading was complete

LIST OF STEVEDORE COMPANIES AND STEVEDORES
compiled by John Hawkins

Palgrave Murphys
Jack Guidon, Paddy Grimes, Harry Jackson and Paddy Fynes

Irish Shipping
Patsy Kelly and Paddy Kelly

R.A. Burkes
Kevin Kelly and Tony Kelly

George Bell
Willie Downey, Eamonn Downey, Tonner Downey and Tom Penstin

Betson Shipping

Doyle Shipping (Carrick Stevedores)
Michael and Phil Carrick

CDL Coal Ships
Willie Byrne and Harry Jackson

Todd Masterson

Nolan Shipping
Gerry Nolan

Dublin Maritime
Bob Fullam, Rollo Fullam and Joe Fullam

Shally Dowd Slag Boats

ACKNOWLEDGEMENTS

Alma Delahunty, John Grogan, Catherine McComish, Abby Lombino, Grace Newton, Brendan Palmer, Liza Philips, Phoebe Randall, Rachel Wernquest, Emma Edwards, Sharon Hogan, Djamel White, Eva Creely, Sandra Hogan, Emmery Llewellyn, Bridie O'Reilly, Katie Bartrand, Orla Lehane and Colm Quearney.

Ringsend & Irishtown Community Centre.

Contributing Artists

Artistic Coordinator: Theresa McKenna

Cover Artwork: Aidan Hickey

Painting 'Two Coalmen' by Margaret Cullen (Mairéad)

Photographs supplied by Dublin Dock Workers Preservation Society.

Full collection available at www.bluemelon.com/alanmartin